1 & 2 Thessalonians

A Digest of Reformed Comment

1 & 2 Thessalonians

A Digest of Reformed Comment

GEOFFREY B. WILSON
**MINISTER OF BIRKBY BAPTIST CHURCH
HUDDERSFIELD**

THE BANNER OF TRUTH TRUST

THE BANNER OF TRUTH TRUST
3 Murrayfield Road, Edinburgh EH12 6EL
P.O. Box 621, Carlisle, Pennsylvania 17013, USA

★

© Geoffrey Backhouse Wilson 1982
First published 1982
ISBN 0 85151 339 5

★

Filmset, printed and bound in Great Britain by
Hazell Watson & Viney Ltd, Aylesbury, Bucks

CONTENTS

PREFACE

In a day when prophetic sensationalism abounds, it is hoped that this book may help to promote a more scriptural understanding of the Lord's return. For though many choose to subordinate exegesis to speculation, reverent students of the Word will always refuse to tarnish the believer's great hope with the theories of men, preferring with Calvin to remain silent when Scripture is silent.

My aim in this series is to simplify and condense the thought of the great commentators on the Epistles for the benefit of a wider circle of readers, and I am indebted to these distinguished authors and their publishers for permission to quote from their works. In this revised edition, the commentary is based on the American Standard Version (1901), published by Thomas Nelson Inc.

It is again a pleasure to record my thanks to Mr. S. M. Houghton M.A. for kindly correcting the typescript, and to the staff of Dr. Williams' Library and New College Library for their generous assistance.

Huddersfield   GEOFFREY WILSON
September, 1981

PREFACE

INTRODUCTION

After leaving Philippi where they had been so 'shamefully treated' by the magistrates [1 *Thess* 2.2; cf *Acts* 16], Paul and Silas took the Egnatian highway through Amphipolis and Apollonia on the hundred mile journey which brought them to the important city of Thessalonica. Ancient Therme was refounded as Thessalonica in 315 BC by Cassander who named it after his wife, a half-sister of Alexander the Great. Strategically situated at the head of the Thermaic Gulf and endowed with a fine harbour, it was the junction of the great land and sea routes between East and West. These natural advantages had secured its prosperity and attracted a large Jewish colony. Thessalonica was also fortunate in its political privileges, for it was the capital of the Roman province of Macedonia (146 BC), and as a 'free' city (42 BC) its citizens had the right to choose their own rulers or 'politarchs'.

It was probably early in AD 50 when Paul and Silas, accompanied by Timothy, first came with the gospel to Thessalonica. Following his usual practice Paul began the mission in the synagogue. Here for three successive sabbaths he sought to show from the Scriptures that the Messiah had to suffer and rise again, and that the fulfilment of Israel's hope was found in the very Jesus he proclaimed. This revolutionary doctrine was believed by some Jews and many of the 'God-fearing' Gentiles,[1], among whom were quite a number of notable women, with the result that they left the synagogue to meet at Jason's house where Paul and Silas continued to instruct them for a few more weeks. But the loss of their prospective converts to these itinerant teachers so enraged the Jews that they soon contrived a way to bring the visit to an abrupt end. With the help of some ruffians they caused a riot in the city, and in the hope of laying hands on Paul and his associates they attacked Jason's house. When they failed to find them, they brought Jason and some fellow-believers before the politarchs, alleging that these men had received the agitators whose seditious claims for another Emperor called Jesus had turned the world upside down! The civic authorities dared not ignore such a serious charge, but in view of the lack of evidence to support it the accused were bound over to keep the peace and then dismissed. It was therefore to remove the threat of any further action against their Thessalonian friends that the missionaries departed by night for Beroea [cf *Acts* 17.1–10].

This apparent desertion of the infant church in the face of persecution greatly distressed Paul, especially as he was forced to leave before its members were thoroughly established in their newly-found faith. From Beroea, where the Jews of Thessalonica were again responsible for the interruption of another promising work, the apostle proceeded alone to Athens. Here he was joined by Timothy [1 *Thess* 3.2], whom he at once sent back to Thessalonica to see how the church was faring in his absence. When Timothy later rejoined Paul in Corinth it was with heartening news of the Thessalonians' firm faith and influential witness.

1. Dissatisfied with what paganism had to offer, such Gentiles were drawn by the teaching of Judaism but repelled by its ritual requirements (cf Morris, *Tyndale Commentary*, p. 12).

But there were also problems of belief and behaviour which largely stemmed from an inadequate grasp of what Paul had taught them about the return of Christ. As unexpected hindrances had so far prevented a further visit, Paul immediately wrote to express his joy in their progress, to rebut the slanders of his Jewish opponents, and to supply what was lacking in their faith. In regard to Christ's promised appearing, some were discouraged lest loved ones who had died would be at a disadvantage as compared with those who were still alive when it happened, while others were encouraged to idleness by their immediate expectation of this event.

Although Paul's first letter evidently served to correct the sexual laxity which is reflected in 1 *Thess* 4.3–8, further reports confirmed that the eschatological perplexities in Thessalonica continued unresolved. Accordingly, this was soon followed by a second letter in which he reminded them of the things that must precede the Lord's return, for the *imminence* of this hope did not imply its *immediate* fulfilment. Meanwhile he commanded them to lead disciplined and useful lives by earning their own bread and minding their own business. Laziness was no sign of a superior spirituality; the slacker who refused to work should not be supplied with free food! His sharp reproof showed that the apostle would not allow any wedge to be driven between their heavenly interest and the practical concerns of everyday living.

As we read these early documents of the Christian Church today, we are inspired by Paul's intense love for his flock and challenged by the Thessalonians' virile faith. And if we discover that the problems they faced were not peculiar to their day, we also realize that the inspired answers they received are valid for all time.

1 THESSALONIANS

CHAPTER ONE

Paul's associates, Silvanus and Timothy, join with him in sending greetings to the church of the Thessalonians [v 1]. They thank God for their faith, love, and patience, for these evident tokens of their election show that the gospel came to them not only in word but also in the Spirit's power and in much assurance [vv 2–5]. The Thessalonians became imitators of their teachers and of the Lord, with the result that their witness was an example to the Christians of Macedonia and Achaia, who reported how they had turned from idols to serve the living God and to wait for his Son from heaven [vv 6–10].

*V*1: **Paul, and Silvanus, and Timothy, unto the church of the Thessalonians in God the Father and the Lord Jesus Christ: Grace to you and peace.**

If this is not Paul's earliest Epistle (probably Galatians was written before it), the greeting is certainly his briefest (only 19 Greek words). This is conventional in form but bears the stamp of its distinctively Christian content. The unusual omission of 'apostle' from the greeting shows that Paul's authority was not in question and that he enjoyed particularly happy relations with the Christians of Macedonia [cf *Phil* 1.1].

Paul, and Silvanus, and Timothy, Paul is clearly the

real author of the letter [cf 2.18; 3.5; 5.27], but Silvanus and Timothy are here named as 'the joint asserters and approvers of the truth contained in it' (James Fergusson). For they both share his concern for the Thessalonians' spiritual progress and also agree on the best means of promoting it. Silas, who was a member of the Jerusalem church and a Roman citizen, replaced Barnabas as Paul's colleague on the second missionary journey [*Acts* 15.40], while Timothy was the young man who joined them at Lystra and was to become the apostle's most trusted lieutenant [*Acts* 16.1].

unto the church of the Thessalonians in God the Father and the Lord Jesus Christ: Having been called out from idolatry to eternal life by the gospel [*v* 9], this company of believers now formed 'the church' whose life was rooted in God and Christ [cf *Col* 3.3] – an expression which distinguishes the Persons even as it affirms their absolute equality.[1] The essence of their faith was in knowing God as their Father and the Lord Jesus Christ as their Redeemer. In the historical Jesus who had died and risen again for their salvation [4.14], they joyfully recognized the Divine Lord and Anointed Deliverer through whom they had been reconciled to God [cf *Acts* 2.36].

Grace to you and peace. As usual Paul's prayer for his readers is that they may be blessed with the grace that brings peace and prosperity to the whole man. 'Grace is the love of God, spontaneous, beautiful, unearned, at work in Jesus Christ for the salvation of sinful men; peace is the effect and fruit in man of the reception of grace' (James Denney).

1. Cf B. B. Warfield, 'God our Father and the Lord Jesus Christ': *Biblical and Theological Studies*, pp 60–78.

*V*2: **We give thanks to God always for you all, making mention** *of you* **in our prayers;**

One old commentator, cited by William Neil, remarks 'There are some prayers in Homer's poems but how few thanksgivings!'. But though such ingratitude is characteristic of paganism [*Rom* 1.21], a constant spirit of thankfulness marks out those who have been made sensible of God's multiplied mercies. Hence Paul, Silas, and Timothy are daily filled with fervent thanksgiving to God as they think of what his grace has wrought in the lives of these Thessalonians. Their prayers for their converts' continuing progress in the faith are pervaded with grateful praise to God because every believer is a standing monument to Divine mercy. This thanksgiving is not therefore a mere rhetorical device intended to win over the readers with fulsome flattery [2.5], but is rather an earnest attempt on the part of the missionaries 'to raise the thoughts of their converts to the God on whom they are wholly dependent, and in consequence to rouse them to fresh efforts' (George Milligan).

*V*3: **remembering without ceasing your work of faith and labour of love and patience of hope in our Lord Jesus Christ, before our God and Father;**

continually bearing in mind your work resulting from faith and (your) exertion prompted by love and (your) endurance inspired by hope in our Lord Jesus Christ in the presence of our God and Father; (Hendriksen) This verse describes the immediate ground of the thanksgiving, while the following verse discloses its ultimate ground ('knowing . . . your election'). The arrangement of the great triad of Christian graces in the ascending

[17]

scale of faith, love, and hope is appropriate in a letter which largely deals with the 'hope' of Christ's return; just as it was natural to assign the dominant position to 'love' in the passage devoted to extolling that grace [1Cor 13.13; cf 5.8; Gal 5.5, 6; Col 1.4, 5].

Here Paul first thanks God for the work that results from faith. Theirs was no barren assent to a dogma [James 2.17], but the dynamic outworking of a life-transforming principle [Gal 5.6]. This work should not be too narrowly defined, though it no doubt included their active propagation of the gospel [v 8]. He next mentions the laborious toil that is prompted by love. As George Findlay says, work points to *the thing done*, as a matter of achievement: labour indicates the *pains spent* in doing it, as matter of exertion. '*Work* may be easy and delightful; *labour* is toilsome; no selfish man will endure it for another's good. Hence *labour* is the test of *love*'. This was a new concept of love which was supremely exemplified by Christ, and for which Christians adopted a new word and made it their own (*agapē*). It is the self-denying, sacrificial love that gives itself unstintingly in the service of others. Finally Paul refers to the endurance that is inspired by hope in our Lord Jesus Christ. This is not the spirit which suffers with resignation; it is the fortitude which meets trials in the certain hope of the final victory at Christ's coming [cf v 6; 3.2–6]. And to speak of this hope naturally brings to mind the day when believers will rejoice in the presence of the God whom they know as their Father [3.13].

V4: knowing, brethren beloved of God, your election,

knowing, 'By the manner of their receiving the gospel, and the evident operation of the graces of God's Spirit, the apostle knew their election of God. We cannot know election as in God's secret decree, but as made manifest in the fruits and effects of it. As there is a knowledge of things *a priori*, when we argue from the cause to the effect, so *a posteriori*, when we argue from the effects to the cause. And thus the apostle came to know their election. Not, we hope it, or conjecture it, but we know it; and not by extraordinary revelation, but by evident outward tokens' (Matthew Poole).

brethren So conscious is Paul of the closeness of this bond with his readers that he uses the word twenty-one times in these epistles. As Leon Morris well says, 'There is a sense in which all men may be thought of as brothers. The fraternity of a club or lodge may be very real. But in the sense that matters, brethren are brethren in Christ. The Christian brotherhood is the fellowship of the redeemed'.

beloved of God, The participle 'beloved' is not in the present tense, 'as though the Thessalonians were simply loved now, in consequence of their newly-acquired Christian worth; it is in the Greek perfect tense, signifying a love existing in the past and realized in the present, the antecedent and foundation of their goodness' (Findlay). [cf 1 *John* 3.1]

your election, The unexplained reference to 'election' advertises the fact that this truth had formed an essential part of Paul's proclamation of the gospel in Thessalonica. Unlike those who take it upon themselves to conceal what God has been pleased to reveal, the apostle always declared the whole counsel of God [*Acts* 20.27], and not simply that part of it which would not offend the autonomy of the natural man. This is an eternal election of God [*Eph* 1.4; cf 2 *Thess* 2.13] to final salvation [*Eph* 1.11], of a people whom He gave to Christ 'before times eternal' [2 *Tim* 1.9; *John* 6.38,39; 17.2–12], without respect to their foreseen faith [*Rom* 9.11], the grand purpose of which is to redound to the glory of his grace [*Eph* 1.6].

*V*5: **how that our gospel came not unto you in word only, but also in power, and in the Holy Spirit, and** *in* **much assurance; even as ye know what manner of men we showed ourselves toward you for your sake.**

because our gospel came not unto you in word only, (ASV margin) Paul knew the Thessalonians to be elect because 'the Spirit was in us who preached [*v* 5], and in you who welcomed the word [*vv* 6–10]. By saying "our gospel came" instead of "we came with the gospel" [2 *Cor* 10.14], Paul puts the emphasis more upon the message as the means of realizing God's call than upon the bearers of the message' (James E. Frame). For though preachers must come and speak the message of salvation [*Rom* 10.14], it needs more than a declaration in 'word only' to bring the dead to life [*Eph* 2.1] 'Our gospel' means that it was theirs by divine commission and personal experience. They had not run without being sent, nor had they idly spoken of things unknown to themselves – two essential qualifications for effective preaching.

but also in power, and in the Holy Spirit, and *in* **much assurance;** Here 'power' (the singular shows that charismatic manifestations are not in view) refers to the clothing of the preachers' words with that vital force which had brought salvation to the Thessalonians [cf *Rom* 1.16; 1 *Cor* 2.4]. This benign power [*contrast* 2 *Thess* 2.9] is always associated with 'the Holy Spirit', whose unique prerogative it is to make the gospel meaningful to men [1 Cor 12.3]. The ambiguity of the final phrase 'in much assurance' is removed in Moffatt's rendering 'with ample conviction on our part'. These preachers were so conscious of the assistance of the Holy Spirit in their ministry that they were fully convinced that God's word would accomplish the work for which He sent it forth]Is 55.11].

even as ye know what manner of men we showed ourselves toward you for your sake. Paul now appeals to what the Thessalonians know of the kind of ministry that he and his companions exercised among them as a sufficient reply to the accusations of their opponents [cf 2.1–12; 17–20]. It seems reasonable to assume that the unbelieving Jews of Thessalonica were responsible for these attacks upon their integrity. Apparently they had said that the missionaries would never return to their deluded converts because they were nothing but wandering teachers who scratched a living by imposing upon the credulous from place to place. Thus they sought to offset the effects of the message they hated by discrediting its messengers.

*V*6: **And ye became imitators of us, and of the Lord, having received the word in much affliction, with joy of the Holy Spirit; 7 so that ye became an ensample to all that believe in Macedonia and in Achaia.**

This shows that the subjective confidence of the preachers was verified by the objective change in their hearers. The verb marks the moment when their changed lives gave visible evidence of their election. The example of Christ's witnesses is placed first because 'the Thessalonians came into contact with the model, Christ, through the model copies of Christ, Paul and his companions. If they had not been attracted by the latter they could not have known the former, the chief attraction. So it is the reflection of Christ in us that today induces others to become Christlike' (R. C. H. Lenski).

when amid great tribulation you welcomed the word with joy imparted by the Holy Spirit, (Hendriksen). The great change effected by the word they so readily received amid the pressures of persecution was also accompanied by the joy of the Holy Spirit. It was never Paul's practice to portray an easy road to heaven, for he knew that all who become imitators of the Lord are called to share in the rejection which He met from an unbelieving world [3.3, 4; *John* 16.33; Acts 14.22; *Phil* 1.29; 2 *Tim* 1.8]. But the early Christians not only expected persecution as the inevitable accompaniment of genuine discipleship, they also received it as a badge of honour with Spirit-inspired joy [Acts 5.41].

so that ye became an ensample to all that believe in Macedonia and in Achaia. The result of their imitation of the Lord was that the Thessalonian church became a 'model' or 'pattern' for imitation to all who believed in the provinces of Macedonia and Achaia. News of their faithful witness in the face of heavy trials had radiated from this important centre to encourage believers throughout both provinces to stand firm. Thus an impressive proof of the power of a living faith in Christ was furnished by the fact that the imitators were now the imitated!

*V*8: **For from you hath sounded forth the word of the Lord, not only in Macedonia and Achaia, but in every place your faith to God-ward is gone forth; so that we need not to speak anything.**

This explains and expands the previous verse. Paul speaks of the gospel, which is the Lord's word to men, as sounding forth from them – the perfect tense indicating not a finished act but a continuing process. Certainly this word did not originate with them, but they had received it so wholeheartedly that its echoes were heard everywhere. Such was the fame of their faith that they had become missionaries to the whole world by way of report!

so that we need not to speak anything. i.e. of your faith in God. 'Where men's deeds speak and commend men, words may be silent. And the apostle might have thought it needful to have divulged these things abroad for the advantage of the gospel, and the examples of others, if he had not been forestalled by the report already spread abroad. The good examples of the people may ease their ministers of some labour in spreading the gospel' (Poole).

*V*9: **For they themselves report concerning us what manner of entering in we had unto you; and how ye turned unto God from idols, to serve a living and true God,**

for they themselves are reporting about us, what kind of entering in we had among you, (Hendriksen) Thus when people keep telling Paul of the success of the Thessalonian mission he can hardly doubt that those it had benefited will know how to deal with the base allegations of his opponents [*v* 5; 2.1–12]. What follows gives the substance of these reports in words that are evidently intended to remind them of the preaching through which they had been delivered from the power of darkness [cf 1 *Cor* 10.19, 20].

and how ye turned unto God The significance of their conversion was seen in their *turning* from idols to *serve* the living God and in *waiting* for the advent of his Son from heaven [*v* 10]. As B. B. Warfield says, 'There are two groups of terms in the New Testament used to express the great change which is experienced by him who enters upon the Christian life. One of these groups includes those terms which describe the change from the manward side, and inform us what part man himself takes in it. The other group includes the terms that 'describe the change from the Godward side, and tell us what part God takes in it. Man repents, makes amendment, and turns unto God; but it is God who renews him, begets him again, quickens or creates him into newness of life. The two groups describe the two sides of the same great occurrence, and must be combined in any complete conception of its nature and implications' (*Selected Shorter Writings*, Vol I, p. 267). So though the Thessalonians did turn to God, they were enabled to do so only because the gospel came to them in the power of the Holy Spirit [*v* 5].

from idols, to serve Pagan belief in a multitude of gods meant that the real power in the world was not found in any of them, but in some sort of fate to which even its deities were subject. As man could not enter into a moral relation with this blank necessity, no Greek or Roman could take in the idea of 'serving' a god (Denney). Hence the liberation of the ancient world from the shackles of its superstition required the apostolic witness to the One Supreme God as its Creator and Redeemer, for it is this alone that enables men to regard the whole of life as a moral service which they owe to him [cf *Rom* 12.1,2]. 'Only the man who has learned to put himself wholly in subjection to God is truly converted to Him' (John Calvin).

a living The absence of the article which is reflected in the literal rendering of the ASV draws attention to the *character* of God, who alone has life in himself, 'and is the author and preserver of life unto others, *Acts* 17.28' (Fergusson), in contrast to the lifeless idols of men's hands which cannot move a finger to help their deluded worshippers [cf *Ps* 115. 4ff; *Is* 40.18ff].

and true God, The meaning is not the true as opposed to the false; the contrast is between the true and the unreal. He is '*very* God, as distinguished from idols and all other false gods, the dreams of the diseased fancy of men, with no substantial existence in the world of realities' (R. C. Trench).

*V*10: **and to wait for his Son from heaven, whom he raised from the dead,** *even* **Jesus, who delivereth us from the wrath to come.**

The word 'to await' occurs only here in the New Testament; it 'implies *sustained* expectation' (Findlay). Paul's use of this intensive word in connection with the hope of Christ's appearing is indeed suggestive. As Matthew Poole well says, 'They believed that he was gone to heaven, and would come again, which are two great articles of the

Christian faith. And though there was nothing in sense or reason, or any tradition, to persuade them of it, yet they believed it upon the apostle's preaching it. And though the time of his coming was unknown to them, yet their faith immediately put them upon waiting for it. And the certain time of his coming is kept secret, that the saints in every age may wait for it. Though he will not come till the end of the world, yet the saints ought to be influenced with the expectation of it in all generations that do precede it'.

whom he raised from the dead, 'The theology of Paul is, that the Father raised the Son from the dead, and this resurrection has an evidential connection with the Sonship and the completion of His earthly work [*Rom* 1.4]' (John Eadie).

Jesus, our Deliverer from the wrath to come. (F. F. Bruce) Although the notion seems so strange to modern ears long accustomed to hearing nothing but the love of God, deliverance from the wrath of God was an essential element in the apostolic preaching of the gospel. Here the Jesus who died to become the Deliverer of his people is shown to be one and the same with the glorified Son whose advent they await in the confidence that God has not appointed them to wrath, but to the obtaining of salvation through him [5.9]. 'For, though the wrath of God is always being revealed to a greater or less extent in the judgments of God that find expression in the providential ordering of human history, the history both of nations and of individuals, it remains true that in His mercy He endures "with much longsuffering the vessels of wrath fitted to destruction" [*Rom* 9.22]. In consequence there must be, and the Bible again and again affirms that there will be, a final day of judgment which will prove a day of full salvation for the believer, but will be a day of uttermost wrath for the wicked' (R. V. G. Tasker, *The Biblical Doctrine of the Wrath of God*, p. 37].

CHAPTER TWO

In refuting the charges brought against the missionaries by their opponents, Paul reminds the Thessalonian Christians of the truthfulness and sincerity of their preaching, of the purity of their conduct, and of their strong affection towards them [vv 1–12]. After having toiled so hard among them, Paul and his companions are thankful to God that the Thessalonians not only received the gospel as the word of God but were also prepared to endure the hardships inflicted upon them by their Jewish persecutors [vv 13–16]. The enforced absence from the beloved converts who are his hope and joy is keenly felt by Paul, who had wished twice to return to them, but Satan hindered him [vv 17–20].

*V*1: **For yourselves, brethren, know our entering in unto you, that it hath not been found vain:**

For you yourselves know, brethren, (RSV) This 'you yourselves' is opposed to the 'they themselves' of 1.9 – the Thessalonians know at first-hand what others are merely reporting about them. For 'you are the ones who experienced it. The people in the provinces talk about it far and wide, they have only heard the story, *you* are the ones who *know*' (Lenski). With this brilliant stroke Paul begins his defence against the attacks of the Jews, for clearly no witnesses were better qualified to vouch for the genuineness of the missionaries' motives and methods than their own converts [2.1–12].

Those who have turned from the futile worship of dumb idols are in the best position to know that the 'entering in' of the preachers was not in vain, i.e. it was not empty of reality and power. Our mission to you was not *empty*, or 'hollow, like a vessel that has nothing in it. This is a litotes which states the matter negatively but intends it positively: "not an empty one" = one filled to the brim with most blessed effects. The perfect "has been" = and still remains so to this day' (Lenski).

*V*2: **but having suffered before and been shamefully treated, as ye know, at Philippi, we waxed bold in our God to speak unto you the gospel of God in much conflict.**

Despite the scarred bodies [*Acts* 16.23] and smarting spirits [*Acts* 16.37] that were the painful badges of their service in Philippi, Paul and Silas entered Thessalonica with the same intense seriousness of purpose with which they had begun their mission in Macedonia. That they were thus undaunted by *injury* and *insult* were credentials sufficient to show the Thessalonians that theirs was not the empty entering in of religious charlatans.

we waxed bold in our God to speak unto you the gospel of God in much conflict. Paul here recalls how they had pursued their commission with the courageous outspokenness born of their confidence in God, for they were supremely conscious of the fact that their message came not from men but from God. This shows us that the gospel is no human expedient to palliate the symptoms of sin; it is God's cure for the fatal condition itself. 'Our age

[29]

can do with the reminder that the Christian faith is not the accumulated wisdom of pious souls, nor the insight of men of religious genius, but the divine plan for dealing with man's sin' (Morris). The apostle's reference to the fierce strife which their ministry had stirred up in Thessalonica was a telling reminder of the cost of remaining faithful in the face of such violent opposition.

*V*3: **For our exhortation** *is* **not of error, nor of uncleanness, nor in guile:**

This evidently reflects the charges that had been made against Paul and his assistants by their enemies. However, these attacks were so contrary to what their converts knew of them from first-hand experience that they called for nothing more than a flat denial to prove their falsity. Indeed, it is because the appeal of their preaching is that of *God's* gospel [*v* 2] – which is the preaching of *God's* word to men with *his* interests at heart – that it could no more spring from 'error' or 'impurity' than it could be carried out in an atmosphere of 'deceit'. 'Their preaching did not spring from some delusion or mistake. Paul was neither fool nor knave, neither deceived nor deceiver. Nor was his mission a sordid attempt to make a good thing out of preaching, the impure motive being either to secure money [cf *greed v* 5 and *v* 9], or to gain a position of importance [*v* 6] and popularity' (James Moffatt). This explanation of the second charge is more consistent with the context than that which restricts it to *sensual* impurity. And though their detractors were certainly not above making the accusation, they were at least astute enough to realize that it could only be greeted with blank incredulity.

*V*4: **but even as we have been approved of God to be**

intrusted with the gospel, so we speak; not as pleasing men, but God who proveth our hearts.

On the contrary, (NIV) Paul refutes these accusations by showing that they did not teach error for God had entrusted them with the message; that their motives were not impure for they had been approved by God; and that their methods were not deceitful for their aim was always to please God, not men.

as we have been approved of God to be intrusted with the gospel, so we speak; As they have been 'attested' (Moffatt) by God to preach the gospel, so it is as tried and trusted men that they habitually tell out the good news. That they so stand approved before God is not due to any innate worthiness of their own, but rests solely upon the grace of God by which they were fitted for the exercise of this commission.

not as pleasing men, but God who proveth our hearts. 'Men be they pleased or displeased, God must not be displeased' (John Trapp). Thus their fidelity to this divine doctrine was the proof of their divine calling, for they preached not to secure the approval of men but to please God [cf Gal 1.10]. 'The "heart", in the language of the Bible, is not the seat of the feelings alone; it is "the inner man", the real self, the centre and meeting-point of all our thoughts, feelings, and resolves. It is there that God proves us: "The Lord looketh upon the heart". No impure motive or crafty expedient, such as might deceive men, escapes Him. The sense of this continual and omniscient scrutiny makes any kind of dishonesty impossible to the Apostle' (Findlay).

*V*5: **For neither at any time were we found using words of flattery, as ye know, not a cloak of covetousness, God is witness;**

Paul can also claim that their behaviour in Thessalonica was in complete conformity with these general principles [*vv* 3, 4]. Their ministry among them had been devoid of flattery, greed [*v* 5], and self-importance [*v* 6]. Such vices certainly belonged to the verbal tricksters of the day, but they were entirely foreign to the ambassadors of Christ. As to their *words*, the Thessalonians knew that they had not come to them 'with cajoling address' (Frame) in order to gain their own ends. And as to their *motives*, God knew that their preaching was not purely 'a pretext for (satisfying) greed' (Arndt-Gingrich). 'In that which was open to men's observation he appealed to their own testimony; but in regard to what was hidden, to whom could he appeal but to God?' (Augustine).

*V*6: **nor seeking glory of men, neither from you nor from others, when we might have claimed authority as apostles of Christ.**

The phrase 'we might have claimed authority' is literally 'being able to be in weight' (cf NEB: 'we might have made our weight felt'). This is the '*weight* of influence which someone enjoys or claims', and it means to 'wield authority, insist on one's importance' (Arndt-Gingrich). Paul's third disclaimer is not that they waived their right to financial support, but that neither in Thessalonica nor elsewhere had they ever come 'seeking' (he does not say 'receiving') honour of men, though as Christ's apostles they had the right to expect it. Since at least Silas and possibly Timothy are included in the term 'apostles', it cannot be used here in its highest meaning of those directly called by Christ, but carries the broader sense of 'missionaries', i.e. those who have been commissioned and sent out by the church [cf *Acts* 13.4].

*V*7: **But we were gentle in the midst of you, as when a nurse cherisheth her own children:**

Far from showing themselves to be flatterers given to greed and self-importance, they had manifested a mildness in their midst which was born of pure unselfishness [*vv* 8, 9, 11]. In spite of the fact that 'babes' (*nēpioi*) is the better attested reading, 'gentle' (*ēpioi*) is to be preferred because it is the only word that makes sense in this context

as when a nurse cherisheth her own children: 'In this metaphor he expresses two points which he had touched upon, viz. that he has sought neither glory nor gain among the Thessalonians. A mother in nursing her child makes no show of authority and does not stand on any dignity. This, says Paul, was his attitude, since he willingly refrained from claiming the honour that was due to him, and undertook any kind of duty without being ruffled or making any show. In the second place, a mother in rearing her children reveals a wonderful and extraordinary love, because she spares no trouble or effort, avoids no care, is not wearied by their coming and going, and gladly even gives her own life blood to be drained' (Calvin).

*V*8: **even so, being affectionately desirous of you, we were well pleased to impart unto you, not the gospel of God only, but also our own souls, because ye were become very dear to us.**

This is a clear statement of the truth embodied in the metaphor of the previous verse. It should be noted that Paul speaks of what they gladly did, and not merely of what they were willing to do. Being filled with yearning for the Thessalonians the missionaries had not come to get but to give, and to give not only the gospel of God but also their own 'souls' (or rather *selves*, i.e. their whole being). Truly their entrance was not in vain [*v* 1], for theirs had not been the lifeless preaching of loveless hearts. It was an *effective* proclamation because it sprang from this total commitment of themselves in love to those whom they were seeking to reach with the gospel. We must learn that such love is the mainspring of evangelism; without it no souls are won for God.

because you had become very dear to us. (RSV) This deep bond of affection had been forged through the preaching and receiving of God's gospel. For when their conversion had shown the Thessalonians to be beloved of God [1.4], they became still more dear in the eyes of God's servants.

*V*9: **For ye remember, brethren, our labour and travail: working night and day, that we might not burden any of you, we preached unto you the gospel of God.**

This reminder that Paul and his companions had not been a burden on the Thessalonians is a further appeal to their own experience. They well knew what a sacrifice these preachers had made in order to bring them the gospel without charge, toiling to the point of weariness and struggling constantly against hardship. The expression 'night and day' (i.e. 'a part of the night, a part of the day, and not all night and all day long' – Lenski) indicates the long hours it cost them to maintain their independence while still discharging their God-given commission. Although Paul would accept help from established churches [cf *Phil* 4.16; 2 *Cor* 11.8], his policy when planting new churches was to pay his own way by working at his trade as a tentmaker [*Acts* 18.3]. This arduous choice at once freed him from the suspicion of making money out of the gospel and proved the purity of his motives in preaching it.

This is the third time that Paul uses the phrase 'the gospel of God' [*vv* 2, 8]. In verse 2 it suggests 'the greatness of the charge entrusted to Paul; here, *the greatness of the boon gratuitously bestowed* on the Thessalonians' (Findlay). 'We preached' means that they proclaimed as heralds *God's* gospel, without amendment or alteration of any kind. As Leon Morris crisply comments, 'The gospel preacher is not at liberty to substitute his view of the need of the moment for the God-given message of the cross'.

*V*10: **Ye are witnesses, and God *also*, how holily and righteously and unblameably we behaved ourselves toward you that believe:**

Ye are witnesses, and God *also*, 'Much they could judge of, and on such points he appeals to them; much they could not judge of, and on such points lying beyond their cognizance he appeals to God' (Eadie).

how holily and righteously and unblameably we behaved ourselves toward you that believe: Not as though the conduct of these heralds was otherwise towards unbelievers, but only the believers in Thessalonica were competent to judge the spiritual nature of their devotion towards them. As if to say, 'Whatever unbelievers may think of us, you who believe our message know very well that the way we lived among you was a confirmation and not a contradiction of that testimony'. On the positive side, 'holily' and 'righteously' describe their behaviour before God and men, while 'unblameably' covers the negative aspect of both these relations (so Ellicott).

*V*11: **as ye know how we** *dealt with* **each one of you, as a father with his own children, exhorting you, and encouraging** *you***, and testifying,** 12 **to the end that ye should walk worthily of God, who calleth you into his own kingdom and glory.**

Paul concludes his apologia with a fresh metaphor which recalls the faithful pastoral care that was given to every convert. 'The Apostle compared himself to *a nurse-mother* [*v* 7] in his tender, gentle affection; now he is *a father* in the fidelity and manly strength of his counsels' (Findlay). The dual nature of this 'exhorting' is specified by 'encouraging' and 'testifying' [cf NEB: 'appealing to you by encouragement, as well as by solemn injunctions']. Thus to encourage and admonish believers is essential for their spiritual progress, which will be in proportion to their grasp of the privileges and the responsibilities of their high calling.

to the end that ye should walk worthily of God, As Findlay points out, a special feature of these Epistles is the continued emphasis which Paul lays on the relation of the Christian believer to God. 'It was *God's* message the apostles of Christ had brought to the Thessalonians [*vv* 2, 9]; "unto *God*, the living and true", they had "turned from their idols to serve" Him [1.9]. They must, therefore, now live a life "worthy *of God*" – worthy of those who have such a God and are His servants and sons'. Our compliance with this lofty demand becomes a practical possibility only through the enabling power of God's calling [cf *Phil* 2.13].

who calleth you into his own kingdom and glory. The present tense is used because God is calling to that which, in its fullest realization, is still future. For though believers are already by grace the subjects of God's kingly rule, they yet await the final manifestation of the kingdom in glory. 'The *glory* to which He calls us is His own eternal glory, of which all the true members of the Messianic kingdom shall be partakers; comp. *Rom* 5.2' (Ellicott).

*V*13: **And for this cause we also thank God without ceasing, that, when ye received from us the word of the message, *even the word* of God, ye accepted *it* not *as* the word of men, but, as it is in truth, the word of God, which also worketh in you that believe.**

And for this reason we on our part thank God without ceasing, (Lightfoot) That the labour of Paul and his colleagues had not been in vain affords occasion for the renewed expression of their constant thankfulness to God. 'We on our part' answers to 'you yourselves' in verse 1, and marks the transition from the teachers to the taught. 'Having appealed to the Thessalonians' experience of them as missionaries, they now thank God for their own experience of the Thessalonians as converts' (Alfred Plummer).

that when you received by tradition from us the

preached word of God, you accepted it not as the word of men, but as what it really is, the word of God, (Ridderbos) This shows us that to change men's hearts requires more than an external hearing of the gospel; they must also welcome it for what it really is, no word of man's devising but the veritable word of God. Now it is because the ascended Lord stands behind the testimony of his apostles that their delivered word is clothed with his authority and can be spoken of as the word of God (so Herman Ridderbos in 'The Canon of the New Testament', *Revelation and the Bible*, p. 194). Hence Paul later urges the Thessalonians to stand fast by holding to the traditions they were taught, 'whether by word, or by epistle of ours' [2 *Thess* 2.15]. For as the revelation granted to the apostles was unique and unrepeatable it soon became necessary to commit to writing the testimony they first circulated in oral form. 'The apostle cannot, therefore, have any successor who can replace him as bearer of the revelation for future generations, but he must continue *himself* to fulfil his function in the Church today: *in* the Church, not *by* the Church, but *by his word*, "through their word" [*John* 17.20], in other words, by his *writings*' (O. Cullmann, 'The Tradition', *The Early Church*, p. 80).

which also worketh in you that believe. 'Also' brings forward a further feature of the heard word, which because of its Divine origin 'also' works powerfully in those who 'believe', the present tense showing the condition for the continuing experience of its working.

*V*14: **For ye, brethren, became imitators of the churches of God which are in Judea in Christ Jesus: for ye also suffered the same things of your own countrymen, even as they did of the Jews;**

The working of this word within them had been proved by their steadfast endurance of persecution, through which they 'became imitators' [1.6] of the Judean Christians who were similarly afflicted. Such unity in tribulation showed the unity of their faith. For it was their common allegiance to and interest in Christ which had aroused the hatred of the unbelieving. The all-important phrase 'in Christ Jesus' thus distinguishes the Christian from other Judean communities which claimed to be 'of God', but which by their rejection of the Messiah had become synagogues of Satan [cf *Rev* 2.9; 3.9].

for ye also suffered the same things of your own countrymen, even as they did of the Jews; The point of the comparison is that both the Jewish Christians of Judea and the Gentile believers at Thessalonica suffered at the hands of their fellow-countrymen. For though the persecution of the Thessalonians was instigated by the Jews, it could not have succeeded without Gentile help [*Acts* 17.5]. Moreover, as the work progressed, the relatives of those converted would not require any encouragement to oppose the teaching which had wrought this unwelcome change in their kith and kin [*Acts* 17.4]. As Denney says, it is the work of God's word to produce a new character, not only distinct from that of the unconverted but antagonistic to it, so that to the extent that we experience the power of God's word, we come into collision with the world that rejects it. This suffering is therefore the seal of faith, for it is a sign that believers are being brought by God 'into fellowship with primitive churches, with apostles and prophets, with the Incarnate Son Himself'. [cf *Heb* 13.12, 13]

V15: **who both killed the Lord Jesus and the prophets,**

and drove out us, and please not God, and are contrary to all men; 16 forbidding us to speak to the Gentiles that they may be saved; to fill up their sins always: but the wrath is come upon them to the uttermost.

This implacable opposition to the gospel by the unbelieving Jews, whether at Thessalonica or in Judea, was nothing new since they killed both the Lord and the prophets, and harried the apostles from place to place. 'The crowning sin of the race is put in the forefront; they slew the Lord, Jesus; but before the Lord came, they had slain His prophets; and after He had gone, they expelled His apostles . . . What we have here is not a burst of temper, though there is undoubtedly strong feeling in it; it is the vehement condemnation, by a man in thorough sympathy with the mind and spirit of God, of the principles on which the Jews as a nation had acted at every period of their history' (Denney). [*Acts* 7.51f; cf *Matt* 21.38; 23.31]

and please not God, and are contrary to all men; forbidding us to speak to the Gentiles that they may be saved; Not merely 'contrary' in the sense in which Tacitus and others condemned the Jews for their inveterate hatred of the Gentiles, but more specifically for their consistent opposition to the salvation of the Gentiles (*Acts* 22.21f]. The gravity of Paul's charge lies in the fact that this hostility was directed against the highest interests of mankind, as was shown by their repeated attempts to silence the preachers of the gospel [cf *Acts* 17.5, 13; 18.12, etc.]

to fill up their sins Paul does not mean that this 'was their intention; neither does he speak ironically; but speaking as he often does from that Divine standpoint at which all results are intended and purposed results, not outside of, but within, the counsel of God, he signifies that this Divine end was being secured by their wickedness' (Denney). [cf *Matt* 23.32]

always: Eadie explains: At all times in their history, when they killed God's messengers to them, they were filling up their sin, though it was far from reaching its fulness; but 'in Christ's time and ours, by putting Him to death and chasing out His apostles, the measure of their iniquity was at length filled up'.

but wrath is come upon them to the uttermost. Although the exact meaning of 'to the uttermost' is uncertain ('fully' or 'finally' are the most likely alternatives), it can be said that the phrase 'marks the issue to which the *wrath* had arrived: it had reached its extreme bound, and would at once pass into inflictive judgments. As the cup of the *sin* had been gradually filling, so had the measures of the divine *wrath*' (Ellicott). In accordance with the words of Christ [*Luke* 21.20ff], Paul saw this wrath as sending the woes that would utterly destroy the apostate system of worship (centred in Temple and Priesthood), which had killed the Lord and spurned the overtures of his grace in the gospel. The hope that Scripture holds out to the Jews therefore does not lie in the re-establishment of what was for ever abolished, but consists in looking upon him 'whom they have pierced' [*Zech* 12.10].

*V*17: **But we, brethren, being bereaved of you for a short season, in presence not in heart, endeavoured the more exceedingly to see your face with great desire:**

A new section begins here in which Paul replies to the charge of fickle desertion made against them by their Jewish persecutors at Thessalonica [2.17–3.13]. In fact so far were they from being indifferent to the welfare of their converts, that only the briefest period following the enforced separation found them filled with the most intense longing to see them again. Feeling thus suddenly bereft of their loved ones made them all the more anxious to seek a reunion, but these efforts had been frustrated by circumstances beyond their control [*v* 18]. In view of all this, how can the Thessalonians believe the slander 'out of sight, out of mind' – that mere physical separation was the sign of spiritual alienation?

V 18: **because we would fain have come unto you, I Paul once and again; and Satan hindered us.**

They had made these endeavours for they *did* wish to return. But as allegations to the contrary depicted Paul as the chief offender, he protests that he had tried 'more than once' (NEB) to re-visit them. The particular circumstances which stood in the way of their return are unknown to us, but behind these checks to their plans Paul could discern the malign opposition of the Evil One himself [cf 2 *Thess* 2.9; 2 *Cor* 12.7]. 'Hindered' is literally 'to *cut a trench*, or *break up a road*, between one's self and an advancing foe, to prevent his progress' (A. R. Fausset), and so the verb vividly conveys Satan's opposition to the progress of the missionaries. For though Satan is always subject to God's overruling, 'within the limits allotted to him he does hinder God's servants' (Morris).

V 19: **For what is our hope, or joy, or crown of**

glorying? Are not even ye, before our Lord Jesus at his coming? 20 For ye are our glory and our joy.

These incredible insinuations are now effectively dismissed by Paul's rhetorical questions which reveal the intensity of his feeling for the Thessalonians. 'They say you mean nothing to me, but I say you mean everything to me!' Paul 'is not speaking here of the prospect of a reward or of any selfish rejoicing or triumph. The Thessalonians are his hope and joy, and the crown of his glory, as a child of its parent. So Chrysostom: *Who would not rejoice in such a multitude of children, and in the goodness of those children?'* (J. B. Lightfoot). Hence this glorying will be a glorying in what the grace of God has wrought in them through his ministry ('yet not I, but the grace of God which was with me' – 1 *Cor* 15.10).

or is it not also you in the presence of our Lord Jesus at his coming? (Eadie) According to most authorities (though not most English versions), 'even' does not express the true force of Paul's *kai* which is more accurately represented by 'also'. What this 'also' implies is well noted by Chrysostom: 'Can you imagine that the Jews are right in asserting that we do not care for you as well as for our other converts?' The word 'coming' (*parousia*) was in secular use as a technical expression for a state visit to a city by a sovereign, whose arrival was marked by the presentation of an appropriate gift. Adolf Deissmann cites a papyrus from the third century B.C. which speaks of contributions for a crown of gold to be presented to the king at his *parousia*. But in contrast to the costly crown expected by earthly monarchs, Paul says that the Thessalonians themselves are 'the crown of rejoicing' which he will present to the Lord at his coming [v 20]. This is the *parousia* of the King, whose arrival will usher in the new age for all his people. There is therefore nothing provisional about the *parousia*!

'Of a development within the limits of the concept, or a duplication or triplication of the event there is nowhere any trace. It is a point of eventuation, not a series of successive events . . . It designates *the momentous event*, and consequently that which it opens up must needs carry a supreme, absolute weight to the religious consciousness. To conceive of Paul as focussing his mind on any phase of relative consummation . . . inevitably would involve his relegating the eternal things to a rank of secondary importance. It would have meant a repetition, or perhaps a continuation, of the Judaistic scheme of thought' (Geerhardus Vos, *The Pauline Eschatology*, p. 76).

For ye are our glory and our joy. Paul discredits the false accusations of the Jews by showing the strength of his feeling for his beloved converts. Since the Thessalonians are even now his glory and joy, they will remain so at the *parousia*, for they will constitute the crown which he will lay at the Lord's feet.

CHAPTER THREE

*Unable to visit Thessalonica himself, Paul recalls how he had
sent Timothy to strengthen and encourage them in their trials,
and expresses his thankfulness for the good report of their progress
received from Timothy on his return [vv 1–10]. He prays that
God will guide him to them, and that the Lord will so cause
them to abound in love that they may be blameless before God
at the Lord's coming [vv 11–13].*

V 1: **Wherefore when we could no longer forbear, we
thought it good to be left behind at Athens alone;**

**So, unable to bear it any longer, I made up my mind
to be left behind at Athens all alone;** (Moffatt). As this
version makes clear, by 'we' Paul here means 'I'. When
Paul came to Athens he sent for Silas and Timothy to join
him there [*Acts* 17.14, 15]. Since Silas was apparently
unable to leave Beroea at once, Timothy's arrival was all
the more welcome. But such was the apostle's anxiety for
the Thessalonians that he willingly parted with him for
their sake. 'He shows that he had greater consideration for
them than for himself by choosing to be left alone rather
than that they should be deserted' (Calvin). The pathos of
this utterance not only gives us some insight into what
Christian fellowship meant to Paul, but also into what it

[45]

meant to pursue his mission without it in a city that was given over to idolatry [*Acts* 17.16].

V2: **and sent Timothy, our brother and God's minister in the gospel of Christ, to establish you, and to comfort *you* concerning your faith;**

and sent Timothy, our brother and fellow-worker with God in the gospel of Christ, (ASV margin) If this is the right reading (cf NEB, NIV), Paul warmly commends Timothy as a brother who is not simply a fellow-worker but God's fellow-worker [1 *Cor* 3.9]. And the sphere in which he works is the gospel of Christ – 'God's great sphere of operation among men. Timothy preached it, and God rendered it efficacious' (Eadie).

in order to strengthen you and to encourage (you) with respect to your faith; (Hendriksen) Knowing their faith was under attack [*v* 3], Paul sent Timothy to strengthen the Thessalonians and to encourage them to remain steadfast. But it was only because God confirmed Timothy's words in their hearts that these were not empty exhortations, void of any blessed results.

V3: **that no man be moved by these afflictions; for yourselves know that hereunto we are appointed.**

so that no one might be shaken (or disturbed) by these afflictions; (Arndt-Gingrich) The purpose of Timothy's mission was therefore to encourage the Thessalonians to 'stand fast' [*v* 8] in the midst of persecution.

for yourselves know that hereunto we are appointed. 'We' here means Paul and the Thessalonians, 'representing at the same time all believers. Those afflictions are not accidental on the one hand, and we do not court them or merit them on the other hand, but our position brings them on us, and God by his grace has set us in that position. Why then be shaken by them, for we cannot avoid them, and when with you we forewarned you of them' (Eadie).

*V*4: **For verily, when we were with you, we told you beforehand that we are to suffer affliction; even as it came to pass, and ye know.**

In fact, when we were with you, we kept telling you that we would be persecuted. And it turned out that way, as you well know. (NIV) A comparison with *Acts* 14.22 shows that it was Paul's policy to teach his converts that these afflictions were an inevitable consequence of their commitment to Christ, for to be forewarned is to be forearmed. As Findlay says, this is an appeal to the *facts* of the case and the *experience* of the readers. 'The reminder should help to prevent the Thessalonian believers from being "shaken amid these afflictions"; what had happened was natural and expected; it is "no strange thing" [1 *Pet* 4.12]'.

*V*5: **For this cause I also, when I could no longer forbear, sent that I might know your faith, lest by any means the tempter had tempted you, and our labour should be in vain.**

For this reason, when I could bear it no longer, I sent that I might know your faith, (RSV) This rounds off what has gone before [*vv* 1, 2]. Paul now gives the most emphatic expression to the anxiety which prompted him to send Timothy; he had to know how their faith was faring under these trials. The fact that he could sum up the whole of their Christian experience in this all-inclusive reference to their faith is highly significant. It shows us that the Christian life is pre-eminently the life of faith, for it is by believing the gospel that the Christian lives.

lest by any means the tempter had tempted you, and our labour should be in vain. At the time Paul sent Timothy he knew that the Thessalonians were faced with the temptation to abandon their faith, though he had no means of knowing whether they had resisted it. Yet by changing from the indicative ('had tempted') to the subjunctive ('our labour should be in vain'), he manages to assure them that even then he was unwilling to believe that his toil had been fruitless – as it would have been if they had succumbed to the temptation. The apostle here attributes the temptation to the activity of the tempter himself [*Matt* 4.3], whose object in tempting men to sin is to prove them to be reprobate. 'Satan's first work is to keep men from believing, his next is to destroy their faith: young converts are commonly most assaulted' (Poole).

*V*6: **But when Timothy came even now unto us from you, and brought us glad tidings of your faith and love, and that ye have good remembrance of us always, longing to see us, even as we also *to see* you;**

But all anxiety was dispelled on Timothy's return to Paul in Corinth (Silas too had arrived from Beroea), and he immediately writes to express his joy in 'the good news' (RSV). There is a fine play on the word, which is nowhere else in the New Testament used of any other but '*the* good news'. 'Timothy's report was, in effect, *gospel* news, as it witnessed to the power of God's message (*the word of God which worketh in you*, 2.13); and it was the best of news to Paul and Silas – a very "gospel" coming to them in return for the Gospel they had brought to the readers [1.5; 2.2 etc.]' (Findlay).

of your faith and love, i.e. 'faith' in God and 'love' for man, which together comprise 'the sum total of godliness' (Calvin).

and that ye have good remembrance of us always, 'a kindly recollection. In his unselfishness the Apostle had not pressed for an inquiry on this point. But Timothy brings additional information: not only have the Thessalonians not lost faith in God and Christ while under persecution; they have not forgotten the founder of their church, nor turned against him as the cause of this trouble, nor even grown cold toward him, their enthusiasm damped by disappointment' (Walter F. Adeney).

longing to see us, even as we also *to see* you; Moreover, Paul was overjoyed to learn that they were as eager to see him as he was to see them, for the bond which united them had made this longing mutual [cf 2.8, 17; 3.10].

*V*7: **for this cause, brethren, we were comforted over you in all our distress and affliction through your faith:**

'For this cause' brings together all that was said in the previous verse. Timothy's report had brought much needed comfort to Paul. It had confirmed that his work in Thessalonica was not wasted, and thus enabled him to rise above the hardship and opposition he faced at Corinth,

[49]

giving him the encouragement to pursue his mission there in the assurance that his labour was not in vain in the Lord [cf *Acts* 18.5].

through your faith: 'It was the faith of the Thessalonians about which Paul had directed Timothy to make inquiry. Now it is their faith that cheers the Apostle. The brotherly love and the kindly remembrance were fruits of this faith. If faith had failed, they would have vanished. Although the Apostle does not here develop his doctrine of faith as in the Epistle to the Romans, even this early Epistle reveals his consciousness of the unique importance of the fundamental grace' (Adeney).

*V*8: **for now we live, if ye stand fast in the Lord.**

Paul seems to have felt that the progress of the gospel in Macedonia and Achaia largely depended upon the success of his work in this key centre [1.8]. And as the failure of that work would have been the death blow to all his hopes, so the report of their faith came to him as a new lease of life that would last for as long as they stood fast in the power of the Lord. The condition upon which Paul's life depended is here expressed by 'if' with the indicative, perhaps to bring out more strongly his confidence that it would certainly be fulfilled (so Milligan). But Paul is thinking of something beyond his own revived energy: the persistence of Thessalonian faith reveals the vitality of the gospel itself, the word at work in believers, ministered by Christ's servants. They 'live' to purpose, in so far as their message lives on in others (Findlay).

*V*9: **For what thanksgiving can we render again unto**

God for you, for all the joy wherewith we joy for your sakes before our God;

These fears for the stability of his beloved brethren in Thessalonica therefore made Paul's joy in the good news of their flourishing faith all the more intense. It is a joy so great that he is unable to return adequate thanks to God for thus granting them the grace of perseverance. 'Paul views everything as coming from God. His first reaction is: "Thank God!": But how can any thanks be commensurate with the gift of joy he and his assistants have received? . . . As though standing in God's presence, Paul and his helpers live and work; from God they receive this as they do every other blessing; their hearts automatically turn to God' (Lenski).

*V*10: **night and day praying exceedingly that we may see your face, and may perfect that which is lacking in your faith?**

This completes the rhetorical question begun in the previous verse. 'Night and day' (i.e. constantly as in 2.9) Paul earnestly beseeches God to open the way for his return. For his joy in the Thessalonians has increased his longing to see them again, not only to rejoice in their presence but also to perfect what was lacking in their faith. Thankful though he was for their vigorous and steadfast faith, Paul was too much of a realist not to recognize that it needed to be supplemented by further instruction and by a more perfect obedience to the principles they had already been taught. In the meantime the teaching and admonition he is about to impart will help to make up some of the more important of these shortcomings [cf 4.1ff and 4.13ff]. 'Though his Epistles might avail towards it, yet his personal presence would do more. There is a peculiar blessing attends oral preaching, more than reading. The like prayer he made with respect to the Romans, and upon the same account also, *Rom* 1.10, 11' (Poole). In the prayer that follows the thought of this verse is repeated; *v* 11 echoes *v* 10a, while *vv* 12, 13 echo *v* 10b, which by its reference to their present spiritual needs serves to introduce the second part of the letter.

*V*11: **Now may our God and Father himself, and our Lord Jesus, direct our way unto you:**

In this remarkable petition Paul jointly invoked 'our God and Father' and 'our Lord Jesus' by using the verb 'direct' in the singular; an association which, since it indicates the Lord's oneness 'with the Father in the prerogative of hearing and answering prayer' (Findlay), also points to his deity (cf 2 *Thess* 2.16 where the names occur in the reverse order). 'Direct' here means to *make a straight path from us to you*, by the levelling or removal of those obstacles with which Satan has obstructed it' (Lightfoot) [cf 2.18].

*V*12: **and the Lord make you to increase and abound in love one toward another, and toward all men, even as we also *do* toward you;**

'But as for *you*, whether we are again privileged to minister to you in person or not, may 'the Lord' (i.e. the Lord Jesus) grant our prayer for your continued growth in grace'. Paul seeks as a gift for his converts from the exalted Lord that outgoing love which abounds and overflows to bless their fellow-believers and their fellow-men, not excluding their persecutors! [5.15; *Matt* 5.44ff.; *Gal* 6.10.] For such love in action is the indispensable evidence of the genuineness of their faith. As Moffatt says, 'No form of *holiness* [v 13] which sits loose to the endless obligations of this *love* will stand the strain of this life or the scrutiny of God's tribunal at the end' [cf *Rom* 13.8–10].

even as we also *do* toward you; 'But why make themselves the model, why not Christ and his supreme love, which is the model for us all: "just as the Lord (loves) you"? Because the Lord is here presented as the source of our love, and because the Thessalonians have seen the love of Paul, Silvanus, and Timothy, actual examples of the love produced by the Lord in the hearts of his true followers. If the Lord filled these three with such love, the Thessalonians will see that the Lord can do this also for them' (Lenski).

*V*13: **to the end he may establish your hearts unblameable in holiness before our God and Father, at the coming of our Lord Jesus with all his saints.**

The purpose of the prayer for love is that Christ may thereby so strengthen their hearts (their inward purposes and desires), that at the judgment-seat of God [Rom 14.10 NIV] these hearts may be found in a blameless state of holiness. And though this is ultimately the work of the Lord, yet it is a work which demands the active co-operation of the believer [cf *Phil* 2.12]. 'The point appears to be that without the strong foundation of love the will might exploit itself in conduct not becoming to the *saint*, that is, specifically, as 4.3–8 suggests, in impurity' (Frame). For selfless *love* is the opposite of the selfish *lust* that satisfies itself at another's expense [4.5].

at the coming of our Lord Jesus with all his saints.

[53]

'With all his saints' is explained by 4.13–18. Findlay says: These are not the *angels* of 2 *Thess* 1.7; the term denotes always with Paul *holy men* [2 *Thess* 1.10]: 'here *the holy dead*, who will "rise first" and whom "God will bring with Him" – with Jesus – when He returns to His people upon earth'. Thus to assure the Thessalonians of the Lord's return with *all* his saints, including their beloved dead whom they feared might miss this great day, would convey much needed comfort to their troubled hearts; whereas a statement about angels would have no relevance to their particular needs. 'The momentous event' (not events!) is therefore a coming *with* the departed saints and a coming *for* the living saints.

CHAPTER FOUR

*Paul exhorts the Thessalonians to live according to God's will,
for he has not called them to be impure but to be holy [vv 1–8].
He further urges them to increase in brotherly love, and to earn
the respect of the unbelieving community by quietly earning an
honest living [vv 9–12]. They must not sorrow as men without
hope for those who had died before the Lord's coming, because
all believers whether living or dead will then be brought together
to share eternal fellowship with the Lord [vv 13–18].*

*V*1: **Finally then, brethren, we beseech and exhort
you in the Lord Jesus, that, as ye received of us how
ye ought to walk and to please God, even as ye do
walk, – that ye abound more and more.**

'Finally' is somewhat misleading as Paul is far from finished [cf *Phil* 3.1]. The expression rather marks the
beginning of the more practical part of the letter and
introduces the exhortation and instruction which is based
on the report brought back by Timothy. The affectionate
term, 'brethren', registers Paul's confidence that as fellow-
believers in Christ the Thessalonians will certainly follow
the course of conduct he now presses upon them, not in
his own name but with all the authority of the Lord who
bought them [1 *Cor* 6.20]. The pattern of living demanded
by the gospel is no strange thing, for he has already

instructed them in it (see 2.13 for comment on 'received'). And though he gladly acknowledges that they are walking in 'the Way' [*Acts* 9.2], they must make it their constant aim to advance more and more in the path of godliness. For the sole object of the believer's walk must be to please God in all things [1 Cor. 10.31]. 'To be pleasing to God appeals to the *gospel* motive for believers, their love for God in the Lord Jesus, and not to the motive of *law*, the fear of punishment . . . to please ourselves in sin is to turn from God, and this involves a serious calamity; the heathen do not even know God [*v* 5], we do' (Lenski).

*V*2: **For ye know what charge we gave you through the Lord Jesus.**

This is a reminder that their conversion bound them over to a life of obedience. For they had been ransomed from the dominion of sin in order to serve the Lord in perfect freedom [*John* 8.36]. The word 'charges' (ASV margin) has a military flavour and 'is strictly used of commands received from a superior and transmitted to others' (W. E. Vine). (cf *Acts* 16.24] What Paul therefore means is that he had delivered these charges to them *on the authority of the Lord Jesus*. An an apostle in living union with Christ, Paul's commission is not limited to recalling the words of Jesus; the absolute authority he claims for these commandments is that of the exalted Lord himself. The magnitude of this claim should make those who parade their fresh revelations today pause and ponder whether they really measure up to it!

*V*3: **For this is the will of God, *even* your sanctification, that ye abstain from fornication;**

Paul now proceeds to deal with what is lacking in their faith [3.10]. As Frame points out, these exhortations are not haphazard, and it appears from 5.14 that three groups are chiefly in mind: 1. *The weak* who were tempted to indulge in impurity [4.3–8]; 2. *the idlers* who were the most disturbing element in the church [4.9–12; 5.12, 13]; 3. *the faint-hearted* who were anxious both about their dead [4.13–18: the only distinctly new teaching in the Epistle], and about their own salvation [5.1–11].

For this is God's will, your sanctification, (Lenski) Paul is not advancing his own ideas; he is enforcing *God's* will. This is not *the* will of God in its entirety, but God's will specifically as it relates to sexual purity [4.3–8]. Sanctification is at once a gift and a demand. It is a *gift* in that believers are objectively holy in Christ [1 *Cor* 1.30]; it is a *demand* in that it is the will of God that they should become subjectively transformed into Christ's likeness [2 *Cor* 3.18]. And of necessity such a demand involves 'the separation of the spirit from all that is impure and polluting, and a renunciation of the sins towards which the desires of the flesh and of the mind lead us' (L. Berkhof).

that you abstain from immorality; (RSV) Every form of sexual vice was so widespread in Greek society (is our present situation so very different?) that the weak were strongly tempted to relapse into the practices they had been accustomed to regard with indifference. 'What they as Christians needed to remember was that consecration to the true and living God was not only religious but ethical. Whether they had actually tumbled into the abyss or were standing on the precipice is not certain. At all events, Paul's warning with its religious sanction and

[57]

practical directions sufficed; we hear nothing of "the weak" in the second letter' (Frame).

*V*4: **that each one of you know how to possess himself of his own vessel in sanctification and honour,** 5 **not in the passion of lust, even as the Gentiles who know not God;**

that each one of you know how to take a wife for himself (RSV) That 'vessel' here means 'wife' [cf 1 *Pet* 3.7] is in accord with rabbinical usage, and is supported by the context which forbids fornication [*v* 3b] and adultery [*v* 6a]. 'It is God's will that every Christian is to know how to act in the matter of sex so as to be pleasing to God [*v* 1]. He is to know that God instituted marriage, that each man is to have his own wife, each woman her own husband (monogamy), that every type of fornication is excluded as being contrary to God's will' (Lenski) [*Gen* 1.28, 2.24; 1 *Cor* 7.2; *Heb* 13.4].

in sanctification and honour; This is the ethical element in which the acquiring of a wife was to take place: 'the union of man and woman was to be in sanctification and honour, not, as in the case of *fornication*, in sin and shame' (C. J. Ellicott).

not in the passion of lust like heathen who do not know God; (RSV) Since it is through their ignorance of God that the heathen sink into such sins, there could be no greater inconsistency than for those who know God to follow the same shameful course of conduct.

*V*6a: **that no man transgress, and wrong his brother in the matter:**

that (no one) go beyond what is proper and defraud his brother in this matter, (Hendriksen) 'In this matter' shows that the same subject is continued. The euphemism is prompted by Paul's delicacy of feeling, but the flagrant violation of the neighbour's rights which he condemns is clearly adultery [*Exod* 20.14, 17]. 'He has well said *not to go beyond*. For to each man God has assigned a wife, and has set bounds to nature, that there may be intercourse with one only; therefore, intercourse with another is transgression and robbery, and the taking of more than belongs to one . . . It is more cruel than any robbery, for we grieve not so much when our wealth is carried off, as when marriage is invaded. Dost thou call him thy brother and defraudest him, and that in things which are forbidden?' (Chrysostom).

*V*6b: **because the Lord is an avenger in all these things, as also we forewarned you and testified.**

Knowing the temptations to licentiousness which surrounded them, Paul had warned the Thessalonians from the beginning, of the fearful consequences of immorality, so that they could not now plead ignorance as an excuse. 'In all these things': in 'everything that concerns the honour of the human person and the sacredness of wedded life; cf *Heb* 13.4 *fornicators and adulterers God will judge* . . . There is no reason to suppose that *Lord* means any other than "the Lord Jesus Christ", through whom God judges the world at the Last Day: cf 2 *Thess* 1.7–9; *Acts* 17.31' (Findlay).

[59]

*V*7: **For God called us not for uncleanness, but in sanctification.**

The second reason Paul advances for living a pure life rests in the nature of God's calling. It is inconceivable that a holy God should call them *for* uncleanness. Merely to express the thought exhibits the enormity of the antinomian abuse of grace [*Rom* 6.1f]. As therefore God is holy [1 *Pet* 1.14–16], so the Christian must never forget that his vocation is *in* sanctification. 'Holiness is to be the pervading element in which the Christian is to move' (Lightfoot) [*Eph* 1.4].

*V*8: **Therefore he that rejecteth, rejecteth not man, but God, who giveth his Holy Spirit unto you.**

The grave consequence of setting aside this instruction provides the third reason for obeying it. For the one who rejects it, rejects not the advice of man but the commandment of God!

who is ever giving His Spirit, the Spirit whose special characteristic is holiness, to dwell within you. (Plummer) A paraphrase which brings out the force of this unusual reference to the Holy Spirit (literally, 'the Spirit of him the holy'). 'Not only did God call the Thessalonians at the first. He is continually breathing His Spirit into them. But the purpose of this is sanctification; the Spirit of God is the Holy Spirit. To live licentiously while receiving this gift is grossly insulting to the Giver. The obligation to purity, growing out of the reception of the Holy Spirit, is similarly urged by the Apostle when writing to the Corinthians: *Know ye not that your body is a* *temple of the Holy Ghost which is in you, which ye have from God?* [1 *Cor* 6.19]' (Adeney).

*V*9: **But concerning love of the brethren ye have no need that one write unto you: for ye yourselves are taught of God to love one another;**

On the subject of love for the brethren, however, Paul is glad to acknowledge that there is no real need to exhort them by *letter* when this grace was so evident in their *lives*. But since he speaks to those not yet made perfect, he urges them to 'abound more and more' [*v* 10]. Brotherly love (*philadelphia*) is a word which is elsewhere used in the literal sense of love for blood brothers and sisters. But in the New Testament it is used of the special love Christians bear towards one another as fellow-members of the family of faith, as those who are conscious of having the same Father in heaven. Such brotherly love is of special import-ance: '1. for it is a testing fruit of regeneration [1 *John* 3.14; 4.8]; 2. its visible existence is a condition of the world's conversion [*John* 17.21]; 3. a token also of true discipleship [*John* 13.35]; 4. while it is obedience to Christ's new commandment, and enforced by his own example [*John* 13.34; 15.17; *Eph* 5.2]; and is essential to the spiritual growth of the church (*Eph* 4.16]' (Eadie).

for ye yourselves are taught of God to love one another; The word 'God-taught' (*theodidaktos*) occurs only here in the New Testament. It has no reference to any external instruction but signifies the spiritual teaching of the heart. For though it was by the word of God that Paul first taught the Thessalonians to love one another, he gratefully recognizes that they were able to learn this

[61]

lesson only because the Holy Spirit had taught it to their hearts [*Is* 54.13; *John* 6.45].

> *Gracious Spirit, Holy Ghost,*
> *Taught by Thee we covet most*
> *Of Thy gifts at Pentecost,*
> > *Holy, heavenly love.*
> > (Christopher Wordsworth)

V 10: **for indeed ye do it toward all the brethren that are in all Macedonia. But we exhort you, brethren, that ye abound more and more;**

As the capital of the province Thessalonica 'was the natural centre of the Macedonian Churches – including Philippi and Beroea, with other communities which had probably sprung up around these principal towns. The Thessalonian Christians were using their position and influence for the good of their brethren around them, and thus giving proof that they had learnt the great lesson of Divine grace' (Findlay). But they must not rest upon this reputation for brotherly love; they must seek to abound in it more and more. Nor is the admonition without special point, for its development shows that what was true of the church as a whole was not true of every member in it [*vv* 10b–12]. When the passage is compared with 2 *Thess* 3.6–15 it appears that Paul has in mind those who had stopped work in the imminent expectation of Christ's coming. This idleness was an abuse of brotherly love. For in neglecting the duty of self-support they relied on others to meet their needs, while the time which should have been taken up with work was spent in meddling with matters in which they had no concern.

*V*11: **and that ye study to be quiet, and to do your own business, and to work with your hands, even as we charged you;**

Make it your ambition to lead a quiet life, (NIV) Paul sees that the source of this disturbance is inward, 'the excitement created in the minds of some by the expectation that the day of the Lord was at hand. With *Lam* 3.26 he might have said: "It is good that a man should hope and quietly wait for the salvation of the Lord" . . . Inward tranquillity once restored, outward idleness and meddlesomeness would cease' (Frame).

to mind your own business (NIV) He first mentions that which most disturbed the peace of the church. This was the idlers' interference with the affairs of others, particularly with the church leaders from whom they had doubtless sought support.

and to work with your hands, just as we told you, (NIV) During the Thessalonian mission Paul had backed this charge with the force of his own example, which certainly gave no encouragement to the Greek tendency to despise manual labour [2 *Thess* 3.8; cf *Mark* 6.3]. 'There can be no better preparation for the coming of Christ than to be faithful in ordinary duties. The man who is doing his work faithfully at the right time is ready to meet Christ. This thought should quiet all feverish apprehension' (E. J. Bicknell).

*V*12: **that ye may walk becomingly toward them that are without, and may have need of nothing.**

The purpose of this exhortation is now stated, for it is by

earning an honest living that they will gain the respect of their pagan neighbours. 'For Christians to be seen neglecting the duty of earning their daily bread while giving themselves up to religious excitement would prejudice their cause in the eyes of the world, which could appreciate the value of sober work, while it could not understand the spiritual pursuits of the new faith' (Adeney).

and be dependent on nobody. (RSV) 'The gospel bids us aim not only at brotherly love, but at independence. Remember the poor, it says; but it says also, Work with your hands, that you may preserve a Christian dignity in relation to the world, and have need of no one' (Denney).

*V*13: **But we would not have you ignorant, brethren, concerning them that fall asleep; that ye sorrow not, even as the rest, who have no hope.**

With his favourite expression for introducing some new instruction [e.g. *Rom* 11.25; 1 *Cor* 10.1; 12.1], Paul now passes to the topic which was exercising the faint-hearted in Thessalonica. As they thought that only those alive at the parousia would be saved, they feared that their brethren who were already dead had forfeited any share in the coming glory. Consequently they mourned for them like pagans who have no hope. The apostle corrects their error in order to comfort them; for there can be no Christian comfort without Christian faith. It is true that sleep is not a distinctively Christian metaphor for death, but in pagan usage the term is not illuminated by any resurrection hope. So Catullus says, 'Suns may set and rise again. When once our brief light has set, one unbroken night of sleep remains'. As Lenski says, 'Behind this word "sleep" and sleeping the pagan sees nothing but his pagan conception of death, to him the word is a mere euphemism. Behind the Christian word lies all the Christian knowledge of the saving facts which actually make death a mere sleep . . . This sleep applies only to the body of the dead believer and not to his soul'. [cf *Luke* 16 –31; 23.43; *Acts* 7.59; 2 *Cor* 5.8; *Phil* 1.23; *Rev* 6.9; 7.9; 20.4]

that ye sorrow not, even as the rest, who have no hope. It is because Paul knows that the Thessalonians have hope through the gospel that he urges them not to sorrow as the unbelieving do. The contrast he draws is not between natural and excessive sorrow, but between Christian hope and pagan sorrow. The finality of death filled the heathen with a feeling of blank despair. It was a sorrow which was unrelieved by any hope of a future reunion with their loved ones. Theocritus makes the representative remark, 'Hopes are among the living, but the dead are without hope'; whereas a Christian inscription in the catacombs begins, 'Alexander is not dead, but he lives above the stars and his body rests in this tomb'.

V 14: **For if we believe that Jesus died and rose again, even so them also that are fallen asleep in Jesus will God bring with him.**

even so them also that are fallen asleep through Jesus will God bring with him. (ASV margin) 'If' suggests no uncertainty but points to the logical consequence of believing that Jesus died and rose again. For though the Thessalonians did not doubt that Jesus had risen from the head, they had not grasped the far-reaching implications of this great event. Accordingly they must realize that not even death can sever the believer's union with Christ whose triumph over the tomb has ensured the resurrection of all who die trusting in him [cf *Rom* 8.31–39]. In fact they have double comfort, for Paul not only gives them to understand that the resurrection of the departed saints was secured by the rising of Jesus, but also states that God will bring them with Jesus at the parousia. As believers who have this one gospel hope, they are not therefore to sorrow for their brethren as do those who are altogether without hope. It is only 'through' Jesus, who deprived death of its sting [1 *Cor* 15.56], that believers can fall asleep in peace. 'It is significant that he does not speak of Christ "sleeping" but uses the word *died*. He died that death which is the wages of sin; and because He endured the full horror implied in that death, He has transformed death for His followers into sleep' (Morris).

*V*15.: **For this we say unto you by the word of the Lord, that we that are alive, that are left unto the coming of the Lord, shall in no wise precede them that are fallen asleep.**

What follows is given on the authority of Christ's own word. It is impossible to determine whether this refers to an otherwise unrecorded saying of Jesus [e.g. *Acts* 20.35], or to a direct revelation made to Paul by the exalted Lord [cf 2 *Cor* 12.1]. Since 'Paul distinguishes the two classes, the living and the dead, he naturally puts himself among those to whom at the moment he belonged, and who as the living and surviving are contrasted with those who had fallen asleep or died. For there will be a like distinction when the Saviour comes; and to describe the one class the apostle employs the present time and says, "we who are alive and remain". If the Advent were to take place just now, the classification would be literally correct. To the mind of the apostle the second coming was ever present and under this aspect he puts himself and his contemporaries in the one category without actually intending to affirm that they should not taste death till the Redeemer should appear. The clause is thus a vivid way of characterizing all the living as represented by himself and the Thessalonians to whom he writes, while the deceased Thessalonian believers represent all who have died before His appearance and coming' (Eadie).

shall in no wise precede them that are fallen asleep. 'So little is there a reason to grieve over those who have fallen asleep. Those who are alive at Christ's Parousia shall not even precede those who have died, to say nothing of the fear that there is no hope for them. The living and those who fell asleep shall together be joined in glory to the glorious Lord' (Lenski).

*V*16: **For the Lord himself shall descend from heaven, with a shout, with the voice of the archangel, and with the trump of God: and the dead in Christ shall rise first; 17 then we that are alive, that are left, shall together with them be caught up in the clouds, to meet the Lord in the air: and so shall we ever be with the Lord.**

For the Lord himself will descend from heaven with a cry of command, (RSV) We should not fail to observe that Paul's account of the parousia is strictly confined to a justification of the assurance that when this takes place the living will have no advantage over the departed. For it is the Lord himself who shall descend from heaven to awaken the bodies of those who fell asleep in him with a resistless word of command [cf *John* 5.28]. As Denney says, 'In that emphatic *Himself* we have the argument of *v* 14 practically repeated: the Lord, it signifies, who knows

[67]

all that are His . . . It is not another who comes, but He to whom all Christian souls have been united for ever' [*Acts* 1.11].

with the archangel's call, and with the sound of the trumpet of God. (RSV) Possibly the call of the archangel, upon whose identity it is idle to speculate, consists of the sounding forth of God's trumpet, but whatever their precise meaning may be, these expressions can hardly be said to lend support to the notion of a *secret* rapture! Hendriksen reminds us that the trumpet was used to summon the people to meet God [*Exod* 19.16, 17], and also to signal their deliverance from oppression [*Zech* 9.14]. 'So also this final trumpet-blast, the signal for the dead to arise, for the living to be changed, and for all the elect to be gathered from the four winds [*Matt* 24.31] to meet the Lord, may well be interpreted as being also the fulfilment of the trumpet-ordinance in *Lev* 25, and, accordingly, as proclaiming liberty throughout the universe for all the children of God, their everlasting jubilee!'

And the dead in Christ will rise first; (RSV) 'This gives us the key to the Apostle's meaning throughout. Being "in Christ", having died as they lived *in Him*, nothing can part them from Him, "neither death nor life" [*Rom* 8.38]. And when He returns in bodily presence, their bodies must rise to meet Him and do Him homage'. They shall rise *first*, but 'not *before the other dead*, as though theirs were a select and separate resurrection [cf John 5.28, 29]; the antithesis is plainly given in the next verse, – "first", i.e. *before the living saints*: "we shall not take precedence of them, but rather they of us" ' (Findlay).

then we who are alive, who are left, shall be caught

up together with them in the clouds to meet the Lord in the air; (RSV) This blessed reunion with the departed, now raised to new life on earth, also implies the transformation of the living [1 *Cor* 15.51] before both are simultaneously snatched up in the clouds – these 'forming the element with which they would be surrounded, and in which they would be borne up' (Ellicott) – to meet their Lord in the air, i.e. the space between heaven and earth. As Paul's purpose here and in 1 *Cor* 15 is to instruct and comfort Christians he says nothing of the destiny of the wicked, but it seems reasonable to assume that this meeting in the air is preparatory to the Lord's return to earth for the final judgment. For in the papyri the word 'meet' was used of the welcome given to a newly arrived magistrate by leading citizens who went out to meet him and escort him back into the city [cf *Acts* 28.15]

and so shall we ever be with the Lord. [cf 5.10] Vos points out that 'the word "ever" excludes the conception of a provisional kingdom' ('The Second Coming of Our Lord and the Millennium', *Redemptive History and Biblical Interpretation*, p. 421). This is all that Paul here says about the future life, and for believers it is enough! 'The entire content and worth of heaven, the entire blessedness of life eternal, is for Paul embraced in the one thought of being united with Jesus, his Saviour and Lord' (W. Bornemann).

*V*18: **Wherefore comfort one another with these words.**

The bereaved Thessalonians would sorrow most of all; the others would want to comfort them. They have genuine comfort to offer which is unlike the empty condolences of the heathen in the face of death:

'Irene to Taonnophris and Philo, good comfort. I was as sorry and wept over the departed one as I wept for Didymas. And all things which were fitting I did, and all mine . . . But, nevertheless, against such things one can do nothing. Therefore comfort one another. Farewell' (*Oxyrhynchus Papyrus No. 115*).

But the apostle's words comfort as nothing else can because they overflow with the real hope that is only given through this authoritative revelation from the Lord who conquered death.

CHAPTER FIVE

Since they know that 'the day of the Lord' would come as a surprise to men at large, the Thessalonians are to be watchful so that they may be found ready for it (vv 1–11). They are to respect their spiritual guides, to live at peace among themselves, to admonish the idle, to help the weak, and to be patient towards all men. They must renounce the old spirit of revenge and do good to all [vv 12–15]. Refusing to quench the Spirit, they must bring everything to the test, and hold fast to the good while abstaining from every form of evil [vv 16–22]. After praying that God will so sanctify them that they may be blameless at Christ's coming, Paul requests their prayers, commands the public reading of the Epistle to the brethren, and concludes with the benediction [vv 23–28].

V 1: **But concerning the times and the seasons, brethren, ye have no need that aught be written unto you.**

Having shown the faint-hearted that their fears for the departed were groundless, Paul next allays their anxiety that the day might find them unprepared to meet Christ [vv 1–11]. Probably the mistaken belief that survival until the parousia was necessary for salvation had not unnaturally quickened the Thessalonians' interest in the date and circumstances of Christ's coming. But as Paul has already taught them that spiritual preparedness does not consist in date-setting and sign-watching, nothing further needs to be written on this point [*v* 2]; what they do need is the encouragement [*v* 11] to live up to the new status [*v* 5] that God has given them through Christ [*vv* 9, 10]. The distinction between the times and the seasons is that the former refers to the duration of the time that must elapse before the advent, while the latter denotes the critical nature of the events that will characterize the end time [cf *Acts* 1.7].

*V*2: **For yourselves know perfectly that the day of the Lord so cometh as a thief in the night.**

There is no need to write to them on this matter because they know very well that the time of the parousia has not been revealed by God. For this will be as sudden and unexpected as the coming of a thief who surprises the householder at night [*Matt* 24.43] It is evident that Paul has in view the one great event which will wind up the present age and usher in the eternal state [2 *Pet* 3.10–13]. For he here identifies Christ's coming with 'the day of the Lord' [cf 2 *Thess* 2.1, 2 where *both* terms are used in the *same* sentence]. 'Some argue that "the day of the Lord" cannot be the hope of the Christian for it is a day of judgment. It is true the term does denote judgment, but not exclusively so, for through this judgment comes the Christian's brightest hope' (Archibald Hughes). It is when the Lord Jesus comes to judge the unbelieving that he also comes to be glorified in his saints [cf 2 *Thess* 1.7–9 with 'in that day', *v* 10].

*V*3: **When they are saying, Peace and safety, then sudden destruction cometh upon them, as travail**

upon a woman with child; and they shall in no wise escape.

This sudden coming of the Lord will take the unbelieving completely by surprise. 'Even though the Lord threatens them with destruction, they have no hesitation in promising themselves peace and every good fortune. And so they fall into this deadly apathy, because they do not see the immediate fulfilment of what the Lord declares will take place. Anything that is not immediately visible to their eyes they consider to be mythical' (Calvin). [*Matt* 24.37ff; 2 *Pet* 3.3ff]

then a sudden (thing) comes upon them, destruction, (Hendriksen) The reader is kept in suspense by Paul's vivid word order: sudden – comes – DESTRUCTION! This is not annihilation; it is 'eternal destruction from the face of the Lord' [2 *Thess* 1.9]. The thought conveyed by the word is therefore that of 'utter and hopeless *ruin*, the loss of all that gives worth to existence' (Milligan). (contrast *Ps* 16.11)

as travail upon a woman with child; and they shall in no wise escape. As the anguish of a woman's birth-pangs is inevitable [*Is* 13.6ff], so the impenitent shall in no wise escape this destruction. 'It still needs emphasis that there are no other alternatives than life with the Lord or eternal loss. One or the other is inevitable' (Morris).

*V*4: **But ye, brethren, are not in darkness, that that day should overtake you as a thief:**

'But ye, brethren' stands in strong contrast to what is said of the unbelieving in the previous verse. 'Since the Thes-

[73]

salonians are "not in darkness", the coming of day will be no terror or surprise to them. The Day of the Lord will not "overtake them as a thief", stealing on them suddenly and despoiling them of their treasures unawares, but it will come to them as the welcome daybreak, full of light and joy. To the wicked and careless, by a sad contradiction, the Day of the Lord will be *night*! it is to them "darkness and not light, – yea, very dark, and no brightness in it" [*Amos* 5.20]. But for "the sons of light" [*v* 5] it is day indeed, and wears its true character' (Findlay).

*V*5: **for ye are all sons of light, and sons of the day: we are not of the night, nor of darkness;**

The Thessalonians need not fear that the day of the Lord will catch them unprepared, for since they are all even *now* 'sons of light' – those who belong to the realm of light – Christ's coming will also prove them to be 'sons of the day', full sharers in the triumph of that day. 'To the believer the boundary-line between darkness and light is the time of his being brought to the knowledge of Christ. Here, rather than at the moment of his dissolution, or of the Second Advent of Christ, is the great change wrought. From this time forward he is living in the light. And the revelation of a future state presents no such contrast of light and darkness as that which he had already passed' (Lightfoot).

we are not of the night, nor of darkness; The tactful change from 'you' to 'we' (i.e. we believers) is itself an argument for obeying the exhortation [*v* 6ff] that logically follows this reminder of the enlightenment they enjoy in Christ. For having been thus delivered from their former state of darkness it would be the height of folly to fall back into the behaviour-patterns which were characteristic of the old life [cf *Rom* 13.12, 13; *Eph* 5.8].

*V*6: **so then let us not sleep, as do the rest, but let us watch and be sober.**

Paul's conclusion is inescapable. Such a great deliverance obliges Christians to live henceforth in the light; it is not for them to sleep as do the rest. ' "Sleep" is natural to those who are "of the night" [comp. *Eph* 5.11–14]; it is symbolic of the insensibility and helplessness that sin produces' (Findlay). But as befits believers, we must be watchful and sober, remaining *spiritually awake* and *morally alert* throughout the period of waiting for the Lord's coming [cf *Matt* 24.42; 25.13; *Mark* 13.35].

*V*7: **For they that sleep sleep in the night; and they that are drunken are drunken in the night.**

'Sleep and drunkenness belong to the night season, it is the natural time for the one, and it is for many reasons taken advantage of for the other. Believers, on the other hand, are to be wakeful and sober, are not to be like the rest, who are of the night in every sense, it being their element and sphere. What is true of sleepers and drunkards literally is true in a higher and more awful sense of those who lack spiritual illumination' (Eadie). [*Luke* 21.34–36]

*V*8: **But let us, since we are of the day, be sober, putting on the breastplate of faith and love; and for a helmet, the hope of salvation.**

It is only because the Thessalonians belong to the day that Paul expects them to behave in this way, for he always recognizes the assurance of salvation as the nerve of all ethical endeavour. 'Be sober' here includes the idea of watchfulness (carried over from *v* 6) and suggests the simile which 'identifies the Christian's "soberness" with that of the soldier under arms and on guard, in whom drunkenness, or sleep, would be a crime' (Findlay).

having put on the breastplate of faith and love, and as an helmet, the hope of salvation. (Ellicott) The change of tense shows that the sobriety enjoined consists in having donned this spiritual armour and in continuing to wear it. Of the three primary graces which appear here in the same order as before (see comment on 1.3), faith and love are the 'breastplate' that protects the heart, while the certain hope of final salvation is the 'helmet' that covers the head. And though, as Calvin says, Paul mentions only two parts of our equipment, 'he omits nothing that relates to spiritual defence, for those who are furnished with faith, love, and hope, will not be caught unarmed in any respect'. [cf *Rom* 13.12; 2 *Cor* 6.7; 10.4; *Eph* 6.13ff]

*V*9: **For God appointed us not unto wrath, but unto the obtaining of salvation through our Lord Jesus Christ,** 10 **who died for us, that, whether we wake or sleep, we should live together with him.**

We have this hope because we know by the choice (see comment on 1.4) and calling [2.12] which made us believers that God did not destine us for wrath (see comment on 1.10), though we were 'by nature children of wrath, even as the rest' [*Eph* 2.3]. The modern refusal to take account of the awful reality of God's anger against sin results in 'a debilitated Christianity, which does not and cannot do what Christ came into the world to do, viz. save men from the wrath to come' (Tasker, *op. cit.*, p 36).

but unto the obtaining of salvation Our salvation is planned, provided, and bestowed by God; yet we have the duty of 'obtaining' it! This salutary reminder of our responsibility to grasp the proferred grace is in line with the exhortation of *vv* 6–8 which calls 'the readers to a wakeful, soldierlike activity, such as will be crowned by the *"winning* of salvation", the glorious end for which "God destined" them when He first "called them to His own kingdom and glory" [2.12]' (Findlay). (cf I *Tim* 6.12)

through our Lord Jesus Christ, 'This is the uniform doctrine of Scripture. Salvation having God for its source, has Christ for its medium (i.e. mediator). Only through Christ is God known and accessible to us, and only through Him are spiritual blessings conferred upon us by God' (Eadie).

who died for us, i.e. for our sins. The simplicity of the reference points to the Thessalonians' familiarity with the doctrine of Christ crucified [cf I *Cor* 2.2]. This salvation is mediated to men 'through our' (note the confessional 'our') 'Lord Jesus Christ', and that, through his sin-atoning death 'for us'. The mention of Christ's death for us in such close connection with the wrath of God is too important to overlook. For it clearly implies that Christ averted that wrath from us by taking it upon himself, thus delivering us from our deserved doom [cf *Rom* 5.9; 2 *Cor* 5.21; *Gal* 3.13].

that, whether we wake or sleep, we should live together with him. Resuming the thread of 4.13–17,

[77]

Paul now assures the Thessalonians that the purpose of Christ's death is that, whether awake or asleep (in the body) at the parousia, 'they shall together live for ever with Him – in His presence, and in communion with Him. Of that life, so blessed and unending, His presence is the primal element and the "chiefest joy" ' (Eadie). [*Rom* 14.8, 9; *2 Cor* 5.8, 9]

*V*11: **Wherefore exhort one another, and build each other up, even as also ye do.**

Paul concludes this section with the exhortation to comfort one another [4.18] and build up each other in the faith. 'This is Biblical edification, namely, increase in knowledge, assurance, spiritual strength. It is this upbuilding which will produce the comfort' (Lenski). But he is careful to acknowledge present attainments as he encourages further progress, and so 'guards himself against seeming rebuke, while he intends but to exhort' (Lightfoot).

*V*12: **But we beseech you, brethren, to know them that labour among you, and are over you in the Lord, and admonish you;**

As it was evidently Paul's practice to ordain elders in every church [*Acts* 14.23], there is no reason to doubt that he refers to those who hold this office. But to persuade the Thessalonians 'to know' (i.e. recognize and respect) them for what they are, he prefers to describe them by the work they do. This is the heavy toil of leading them in the Lord and admonishing them [cf *Col* 1.28], 'by the word of encouragement, when this is sufficient, but also by that of remonstrance, of reproof, of blame, where these may be required' (Trench).

*V*13: **and to esteem them exceeding highly in love for their work's sake. Be at peace among yourselves.**

As Calvin says, This work 'is the edification of the Church, the eternal salvation of souls, the restoration of the world, and in short the kingdom of God and Christ. The excellence and splendour of this work are beyond value. We are, therefore, to think highly of those whom God makes ministers of so great a task'. But he goes on to observe that Paul's description of how this work is to be done [*v* 12] shows that 'he certainly does not honour the lazy and the wicked, nor does he point to them as being worthy of it'.

Be at peace among yourselves. This appeal is closely connected with the last. Paul's meaning is that 'the general "peace" is to be kept through affectionate loyalty to the approved leaders; it was disturbed by the *idlers*, whom the Church-officers had to "admonish" [*vv* 12, 14]' (Findlay). [cf 4.11; 2 *Thess* 3.6–15]

*V*14: **And we exhort you, brethren, admonish the disorderly, encourage the fainthearted, support the weak,**

Further we urge you, brothers, warn the idlers, encourage the faint-hearted, cling to the weak. (Frame) Some have thought that this is a special charge to the elders of the church, but there is no change of address (cf 'brethren', *v* 12). Ministry is not the monopoly of a special class; the members themselves have a ministry to fulfil to those of their number who are in need of warning, encouragement, and support. The *loafers*, who refuse to work [4.11, 12], are not to be supported in their idleness by the brethren, who are to join their leaders in warning them. On the other hand, they must encourage the *faint-hearted* who were worried about their dead [4.13–18] and also about their own salvation [5.1–11]. Finally, they must not despise but help (cling to) the *weak*, i.e. those who were tempted to lapse into immorality [4.2–8]. It seems reasonable to accept Frame's classification as substantially correct, even if it is perhaps a little too neat to be exact. For example, it is more than likely that the last group would include some who were spiritually immature rather than morally weak.

*V*14b: **be longsuffering toward all. 15 See that none render unto any one evil for evil; but always follow after that which is good, one toward another, and toward all.**

'Longsuffering toward all means not only toward all in the three groups mentioned but toward all, including even outsiders, who may be very trying at times because of their hostile actions. The verb means to hold out long before taking action; God himself is longsuffering toward us' (Lenski).

See that none render unto any one evil for evil; Cf *Rom* 12.17; 1 *Pet* 3.9. Lightfoot thinks that the repetition of the same phrase 'in all three passages would seem to point to some saying of our Lord as the original'. Be that as it may, the expression certainly reproduces the teaching of Jesus [*Matt* 5.44], who also fully exemplified it in his life [1 *Pet* 2.23].

but always keep pursuing the thing that is good (in the sense of beneficial) **in regard to one another and in**

regard to all. (Lenski) But to avoid retaliation is not enough; all resentment is to be extinguished by the love that eagerly seeks to repay evil with good. For if they would not be overcome of evil, they must 'overcome evil with good' [*Rom* 12.19–21].

*V*16: **Rejoice always;** 17 **pray without ceasing;** 18 **in everything gives thanks: for this is the will of God in Christ Jesus to you-ward.**

Since the duties enjoined in these three pregnant precepts are always binding upon believers Denney aptly refers to them as 'the standing orders of the gospel'. They are concerned with the inner motivation that gives Christian conduct its distinctive stamp.

Rejoice always; 'The joy to which they are exhorted even amidst persecution and suffering is no merely natural joy. It is one of the fruits of the Spirit [*Gal* 5.22; *Rom* 14.17; cf *Acts* 2.46]. It is in no way incompatible with loss and suffering [*Acts* 5.41; *Rom* 5.3; 2 *Cor* 6.10]. In his letter to the other Macedonian Church Paul not only exhorts them to rejoice, but practises joy himself even in prison, when outward circumstances might well have caused discouragement [*Phil* 1.4, 18; 4.4, 10, etc]. This joy even in the midst of pain and persecution was one of the great marks of primitive Christianity, which amazed the heathen world, and attracted men to Christ' (Bicknell).

pray without ceasing; Perpetual prayer in any formal sense is obviously impossible. The meaning is that believers are so to cultivate a spirit of constant prayerfulness that their whole lives will be permeated by the presence of God. 'It is not in the moving of the lips, but in the elevation of the heart to God, that the essence of prayer consists. Thus amidst the commonest duties and recreations of life it is still possible to be engaged in prayer' (Lightfoot). [*Rom* 12.12; *Eph* 6.18]

in everything give thanks: Eadie notes that this precept 'is universal in sphere, as the two before it are continuous in time'. As even the most adverse circumstances must work together for the believer's good [*Rom* 8.28], there is no situation to which he should not respond by giving thanks to God [cf *Acts* 16.25]. Such gratitude is the fruit of grace and it stands in marked contrast to the thankless-ness that characterizes the heathen [*Rom* 1.21].

for this is the will of God in Christ Jesus to you-ward. They should always rejoice, ceaselessly pray, and in all circumstances give thanks, because '*this* is (the) will of God' – here the absence of the article limits the reference to this particular part of the divine will. 'The will is made known in Christ, and it is in Christ that men are given the dynamic that enables them to carry out that divine will' (Morris).

*V*19: **Quench not the Spirit; 20 despise not prophe-syings; 21 prove all things; hold fast that which is good; 22 abstain from every form of evil.**

Do not quench the Spirit, do not despise prophesy-ing, but test everything; (RSV) Since fire is associated with the power of the Spirit [*Matt* 3.11; *Acts* 2.3; cf 2 *Tim* 1.6 ASV margin: 'stir into flame the gift of God, which is in thee'], so to smother the Spirit's work is to quench that holy fire. The Thessalonians must not thus suppress the extraordinary operations of the Spirit in their midst. In particular, they are not to despise the gift of prophecy [1 *Cor* 12.28], which was primarily the forth-telling [*Eph* 3.5], and occasionally the fore-telling of the divine will [*Acts* 11.28; 21.11], in intelligible speech [1 *Cor* 14.1–6] under the immediate inspiration of the Spirit. It was by means of these revelations that God was pleased to instruct [1 *Cor* 14.3] and guide [*Acts* 13.1–3] the early church before the canon of Scripture was complete. But because in such oral communications there was always the danger of receiving pseudo-prophecy as a genuine utterance of the Spirit, they are also to put all prophesying to the test by exercising their powers of spiritual discernment [1 *Cor* 12.10; 1 *John* 4.1]. It may well be that the abuse of this gift in Thessalonica by enthusiasts who predicted the immediate return of Christ had tempted the more sober-minded to dismiss it as of no value, hence the need for this corrective.

hold fast what is good, abstain from every form of evil. (RSV) What must result from the testing of every manifestation of prophecy is now set forth. Positively, they are to hold fast to the good, the one beautiful and genuine work of the Spirit which makes for the building up of the church [1 *Cor* 14.12]. Negatively, they are to reject every kind of evil, refusing to be ensnared by any 'revelation' which has been proved counterfeit.

*V*23: **And the God of peace himself sanctify you wholly; and may your spirit and soul and body be preserved entire, without blame at the coming of our Lord Jesus Christ.**

As the preceding exhortations can only be fulfilled in

God's strength [*Phil* 2.13], Paul now concludes with the prayer that he, who is known as 'the God of peace' through the gospel of redeeming grace [*Acts* 10.36; *Rom* 5.1; *Col* 1.20], will himself so sanctify the Thessalonians that no part of their being falls short of entire consecration to him. Clearly this is no piecemeal sanctification effected by human effort, for the radical completeness of the holiness required demands God for its Author [*v* 24].

However, 'It is a thing not yet in possession but in petition . . . Paul though promising this perfection as the certain heritage of every Christian man, presents it as a matter of hope, not yet seen; not as a matter of experience, already enjoyed . . . He openly declares, indeed, the term of our imperfection – the point of entrance into our perfection . . . *at the coming of our Lord Jesus Christ*'. Meanwhile 'we are fighting the good fight; we are running the race. The prize is yonder . . . To us it is a weary process. But it is God's way. And He does all things well' (B. B. Warfield, 'Entire Sanctification', *Perfectionism*, pp. 462–464).

and may your spirit and soul and body be preserved entire, Findlay notes that 'wholly', 'implying a totality from which no part is excluded', is now followed by a synonym 'entire' that denotes 'an integrity in which each part has its due place and proportion'. Although some have appealed to this text to justify the view that man is a threefold being, one might as well cite *Mark* 12.30 as the proof of a fourfold doctrine (F. F. Bruce). Indeed it is quite unwarranted to read a formal definition of the nature of man into Paul's words here when elsewhere he speaks in terms of the duality of man's existence [cf *Rom* 8.10; 1 *Cor* 5.5; 7.34; 2 *Cor* 7.1; *Eph* 2.3; *Col* 2.5]. Rather it is the apostle's fervency in prayer that accounts for this fulness of expression. It means that no part of man's life, outward or inward, whether the latter is considered in its 'God-conscious' ('spirit') or its 'self-conscious' ('soul') aspect, is to remain outside the scope of God's sanctifying power (Bruce). 'Be preserved' stands at the end of the sentence for emphasis in the Greek, and like 'entire' is in the singular, as spirit, soul, and body form one whole man.

without blame at the coming of our Lord Jesus Christ. Since God could not *keep* otherwise than blamelessly, the thought is that they may be found blamelessly *entire* at Christ's coming, being thus made fit to stand in the day of judgment and to share in the glory then to be revealed [*Rom* 8.23; *Phil* 3.21]. Milligan notes the interesting fact that the word 'without blame', which in the New Testament is confined to this Epistle, has been found inscribed on certain tombs in Thessalonica.

*V*24: **Faithful is he that calleth you, who will also do it.**

The assurance that the foregoing prayer is no idle wish but a certain hope is firmly grounded in the character of God. It is an invincible confidence because it relies and reckons upon the faithfulness of God as the caller who never fails to complete his covenant engagements [*Num* 23.19, 20; *Rom* 8.28–30; *Phil* 1.6]. Such an assurance must never lead to a presumptuous security in sin, for the true reception of God's grace is always marked by the obedience through which the believer makes his 'calling and election sure' [cf *2 Pet* 1.5–11]. On the other hand, it would be cold comfort indeed to take our ever imperfect obedience as the measure of our assurance. For the supreme object of our hope is the faithful God who guarantees our participation in his great salvation. As Leon Morris well says, 'It is profoundly satisfying to the believer that in the last resort what matters is not his feeble hold on God, but God's strong grip on him [cf *John* 10.28f]'.

*V*25: **Brethren, pray for us also.** (ASV margin)

The addition of 'also' certainly gives an appropriate meaning. As we have just prayed for you [*v* 23], so do you 'also' remember us in your prayers. Although an apostle of Christ, it was never above Paul to ask for the prayers of his readers [cf *Rom* 15.30; *Eph* 6.19; *Col* 4.3; 2 *Thess* 3.1], for he knew that the superhuman demands which were daily made upon him called for nothing less than the impartation of supernatural strength. This is therefore no perfunctory request, but an urgent entreaty to be upheld before the throne of grace by his 'brethren', his fellow-members in the household of faith.

*V*26: **Salute all the brethren with a holy kiss.**

Since Paul loves all who love the Lord Jesus [1 *Cor* 16.22, 24], he sends his final greeting to *all* the members of the church, thus ensuring that no one is overlooked. As Chrysostom says, 'Because being absent he could not greet them with the kiss, he greets them through others, as when we say: Kiss him for me'. This is the 'holy' kiss which is exchanged between those who belong to the holy community as the sign of their Christian love for one another. What was then the normal mode of greeting soon proved open to abuse so that the practice became the subject of numerous regulations in early Councils, and was eventually abandoned in the West during the thirteenth century. Today in our less demonstrative society the same feeling of Christian love may be conveyed, without giving any cause for offence, by a warm handshake (cf Phillips' paraphrase: 'Give a handshake all round among the brotherhood').

*V*27: **I adjure you by the Lord that this epistle be read unto all the brethren.**

If Paul at this point took the pen from his amanuensis to add the last words in his own hand [cf 2 *Thess* 3.17], this would account for the change from the plural to the first person singular. The unexpected solemnity of the charge has provoked much discussion. But when it is remembered that the letter was sent to meet the needs of a situation he could not deal with in person [2.17f], his insistence that it be read to *all* becomes understandable – otherwise the purpose for which it was written would not be achieved [3.10]. Behind this command there is the apostle's conviction that these words would minister grace to the congregation as it met for worship [*Col* 4.16], and the practice doubtless marked the first stage in the Church's recognition of the canonicity of the New Testament writings [2 *Tim* 3.16].

*V*28: **The grace of our Lord Jesus Christ be with you.**

As always with Paul the farewell is a benediction. He prays that 'the grace' – a favourite word and the keynote of his theology – 'of our Lord Jesus Christ' may be with them. He begins and ends all his Epistles on this note of grace, for the grace that is in Christ is their Alpha and their Omega, their first word and their last. 'Whatever God has to say to us – and in all the New Testament letters there are things that search the heart and make it quake – begins and ends with grace . . . All that God has been to man in Jesus Christ is summed up in it: all His gentleness and patience, all the holy passion of His love, is gathered up in grace. What more could one soul wish for another than that the grace of the Lord Jesus Christ should be with it?' (Denney).

2 THESSALONIANS

CHAPTER ONE

*After the greeting, Paul thanks God for the Thessalonians'
progress in faith and love, and especially for their patience in
suffering [vv 1–4]. But the parousia which will bring retribution
to their persecutors will also be the day when Christ comes to be
glorified in his saints [vv 5–10]. And with that goal in view,
Paul prays that God will fulfil his gracious purpose in them [vv
11, 12]*

*V*1: **Paul, and Silvanus, and Timothy, unto the
church of the Thessalonians in God our Father and
the Lord Jesus Christ; 2 Grace to you and peace from
God the Father and the Lord Jesus Christ.**

The address and greeting differ from the form followed in
the first Epistle in only two particulars. 1. Here God is
called 'our Father', which shows that Paul is thinking of
God as the Father of all believers [*Rom* 8.14–17], ra†her
than as the Father of the Lord Jesus Christ. 2. The added
words 'from God the Father and the Lord Jesus Christ'
make it plain that the Father and Christ are together the
one source of grace and peace. That such a construction
could be used without comment not only implies the
writer's belief in the deity of Christ, but also takes the
readers' acknowledgement of it for granted.

*V*3: **We are bound to give thanks to God always for you, brethren, even as it is meet, for that your faith groweth exceedingly, and the love of each one of you all toward one another aboundeth;**

We are obliged to give thanks to God always for you, brothers, as is fitting, (Hendriksen) Paul, Silas, and Timothy feel impelled as a matter of debt always to thank God for the grace which has made the Thessalonians their brethren in Christ. Moreover, this sense of personal obligation was fittingly in accord with their remarkable spiritual progress [cf *Phil* 1.7]. The word 'groweth exceedingly' (*huperauxanō*) affords another instance of Paul's fondness for compounds beginning with *huper*, and is suitably applied to faith since it suggest a vigorous organic growth. No less appropriate is his choice of 'aboundeth' to express the diffusive, or expansive character of their love for one another (Lightfoot). And in their flourishing faith and abounding love Paul saw the encouraging evidence that his prayer for them was already being answered [1 *Thess* 3.10, 12]. As the apostle often speaks of faith and love without 'hope [1 *Thess* 3.6; *Gal* 5.6; *Col* 1.4; *Eph* 1.15, etc.] there is no need to account for its absence here, though their endurance under persecution implies it [*v* 4].

*V*4: **so that we ourselves glory in you in the churches of God for your patience and faith in all your persecutions and in the afflictions which ye endure;**

From 1 *Thess* 1.8f it appears that up to a certain point the missionaries 'refrained from speaking publicly of the success of their mission to Thessalonica, which had advertised itself in the best possible way; but now, out of gratitude to God, and from the sense of what is due to their

Thessalonian brethren, they can no longer refrain: "while others have been telling about our work, we *ourselves* are now constrained to glory in it" ' (Findlay). Paul's words here show that the church which had been born in a storm of persecution was still bravely bearing up with unwavering faith under the continuing opposition and attacks of the unbelieving.

V 5: **which is a manifest token of the righteous judgment of God; to the end that ye may be counted worthy of the kingdom of God, for which ye also suffer:**

One thought suggests another, so that the sentence is stretched to the end of *v* 10. This brave patience and faith in the endurance of these persecutions is seen by Paul as a sure token of the righteousness of God's judgment at the Great Assize when all the injustices of the present life shall be put right [cf *Phil* 1.28]. Leon Morris points out that 'to be counted worthy' is akin to the great Pauline word 'to justify', and does not mean 'to make worthy' but 'to declare worthy'. Although this implies that the attainment of the kingdom is the fruit of grace, the declaration of their worthiness to enter it is no mere legal fiction, but is in complete accord with the facts of the case. In other words, the reality of the Thessalonians' present justification [*Rom* 3.24, 26] is demonstrated by their willingness to suffer 'for righteousness' sake' [*Matt* 5.10]. Such suffering is not only the natural consequence of their commitment to Christ [*Phil* 1.29], but it also brings them into fellowship with Paul and his colleagues who are enduring the same things on behalf of the kingdom of God. And since Christians are here taught to regard persecution as an anticipation of their vindication by God on the day of judgment, they should never be discouraged by it.

*V*6: **if so be that it is a righteous thing with God to recompense affliction to them that afflict you, ,7a and to you that are afflicted rest with us,**

'If so be' implies no doubt but confirms the reality, meaning 'as it certainly is'. What Paul is at pains to emphasize is the absolute righteousness of God in the final judgment. Then all present wrongs suffered in the service of God shall be righted in the just punishment of their persecutors. In that day the vast question mark which this conduct has put against the justice of God will receive the answer it deserves [*Matt* 7.2]. This is what these evil men 'demand of God by their actions, demand again and again, and God would not be righteous if he did not meet this demand upon his righteousness' (Lenski). But for the Thessalonians who are now enduring the pressures of persecution, this judgment will bring the relief of that eternal rest which has been won for them by the justifying righteousness of Christ. 'With us' is a typically Pauline touch and conveys the encouraging assurance that fellowship in suffering must lead to fellowship in glory.

*V*7b: **at the revelation of the Lord Jesus from heaven with the angels of his power in flaming fire, 8 rendering vengeance to them that know not God, and to them that obey not the gospel of our Lord Jesus: 9 who shall suffer punishment, *even* eternal destruction from the face of the Lord and from the glory of his might, 10 when he shall come to be glorified in his saints, and to be marvelled at in all them that**

believed (because our testimony unto you was believed) in that day.

This section has a rhythmic structure, which some regard as an indication that Paul is quoting a hymn or adapting an apocalypse to Christian use, but it rather suggests that he viewed the Lord's advent with prophetic exultation.

at the revelation of the Lord Jesus from heaven with the angels of his power in flaming fire, The final justification of God [*Rom* 2.5] will be made manifest to all at 'the revelation' or unveiling of the Lord Jesus. Vos notes that whereas the term *parousia* chiefly concerns believers, the militant effect of the advent upon the disobedient is to the forefront in *apocalypsis* (revelation). In relation to believers 'the appearance of Christ will partake of the character of a "revelation", inasmuch as his glory has not been visibly disclosed to them before' (*The Pauline Eschatology*, p. 79). This is the momentary, miraculous descent of the Lord 'from heaven', attended by 'the angels' who show forth his mighty power, and clothed 'in flaming fire' which is his 'awful robe of glory' (Findlay). In so freely applying to Jesus language that recalls the glorious manifestations of God under the Old Covenant [*Exod* 3.2; 19.18], Paul shows that the same burning holiness will characterize the revelation of the divine Son from heaven.

rendering vengeance to them that know not God, and to them that obey not the gospel of our Lord Jesus: 'Vengeance' must not be confused with the vindictiveness of human passion, for the Lord comes to render the retribution which the rebellious deserve. As Findlay says, 'It is the inflicting of *full justice* on the criminal – nothing more, nothing less'. Many maintain that 'them that know not God' refers to the Gentiles, while 'them that obey not the gospel' points to the Jews; but it is preferable to regard the expressions as virtually synonymous, with the second merely serving to enhance the meaning of the first. 'So conceived, the two form one extended category including, with the Thessalonian oppressors, all who in their estrangement from God [cf *Eph* 4.18] disobey His message conveyed in the Gospel of Christ, their disobedience being the sequence and full expression of a wilful ignorance' (Findlay).

who shall suffer punishment, *even* **eternal destruction from the face of the Lord and from the glory of his might,** 'Shall suffer punishment' means 'will pay the penalty'. Such persecutors of God's people will pay the just penalty for their misdeeds. As this punishment is 'destruction', the utter loss of blessedness which is entailed in their perpetual banishment from the presence of the Lord, it is the continuation without hope of the most 'unauthentic' existence imaginable – a ruin as 'everlasting' as the bliss of the redeemed [*Matt* 25.46]. Thus subject to the torment of endless remorse the persecutors will be shut out from the 'glory' of the Lord's might which the salvation of the persecuted so fully reflects [*v* 10]. 'If the gospel, as conceived in the New Testament, has any character at all, it has the character of finality. It is God's *last word* to men. And the consequences of accepting or rejecting it are final; it opens no prospect beyond the life on the one hand, and the death on the other, which are the results of obedience and disobedience . . . Those who stubbornly refuse to submit to the gospel, and to love and obey Jesus Christ, incur at the Last Advent an infinite and irreparable loss. They pass into a night on which no morning dawns' (Denney).

when he shall come to be glorified in his saints, and to be marvelled at in all them that believed (because our testimony unto you was believed) in that day. These two parallel phrases set forth the significance of the advent for those who by grace have put their trust in Christ. The first means that Christ will be glorified 'in' the persons of his 'saints' whose transformation will perfectly mirror his own glory [2 *Cor* 3.18; I *John* 3.2]; the second that Christ will be the object of admiring wonder in 'all' – in every one of those who 'believed'! The aorist tense looks back to the decisive act of faith which has made them sharers in the splendours of 'that day'. Paul's parenthesis assures the much tried Thessalonians that they too will be among this favoured company, because their testimony ('our' includes Silas and Timothy) to the saving truths of the gospel was believed by them. Since the teaching of the apostle here is that the same day which seals the doom of the ungodly also secures the final salvation of all believers, his words clearly rule out the unscriptural notion that the coming of the Lord is in two quite separate stages. 'It is evident that Paul mentions no interval between the time of deliverance and the time of retribution. No period of years elapses. The "rest" and the "destruction" follow in quick succession' (Charles R. Erdman).

*V*11: **To which end we also pray always for you, that our God may count you worthy of your calling, and fulfil every desire of goodness and *every* work of faith, with power;**

With this glorious end in view the missionaries not only thank God for the Thessalonians (1.3ff), but also constantly

[97]

pray that he may count them worthy of his call to salvation on that day (*v* 10).

and that he by (his) power may bring to fulfilment (your) every resolve prompted by goodness and (your every) work resulting from faith. (Hendriksen) God having thus begun a good work in them, they ask that he may bring it to completion by the continued exercise of his mighty power [1 *Thess* 5.24]. And it is because believers are bidden to respond to what the grace of God must first work in them that the petition is also an implied exhortation [*Phil* 2.13]. Accordingly, they must fulfil every resolve that proceeds from goodness and finish every work begotten by faith. As many have remarked, the best commentary on this prayer is the Easter Collect of the Anglican Church: 'We humbly beseech Thee, that, as by Thy special grace preventing (i.e. preceding) us, Thou dost put into our minds good desires, so by Thy continual help we may bring the same to good effect'.

V 12: **that the name of our Lord Jesus may be glorified in you, and ye in him, according to the grace of our God and the Lord Jesus Christ.**

What they ask God to accomplish in the Thessalonians is directed to one end. It is that 'the name of our Lord Jesus' may be glorified 'in' them, and they 'in' him. For as the last day will reveal the full meaning of their union with Christ, so this will bring its revenue of eternal glory to him 'whose name salvation is'. This "name" is "glorified", when its full import is recognized, and the worship which it requires is paid to Him who bears it. So in *Phil* 2.9, we read how the work and sufferings of Christ will have their consummation when "in *the name of Jesus* every knee shall bow, and every tongue confess that Jesus Christ is *Lord*!'' ' (Findlay). All who are then found 'in him' shall share in his glory, even as 'servants come in for a share of the honour of the master whose livery they wear' (Adeney).

according to the grace of our God and the Lord Jesus Christ. The acknowledgement of this grace as 'the source, whence all glorification springs', affords another instance of Paul's anxiety to exclude human merit (Lightfoot). That any of the sons of Adam's race are brought to glory is solely due to the undeserved favour of 'our God' and 'the Lord Jesus Christ', who are therefore worthy of all the praise.

CHAPTER TWO

In correcting the mistaken notion that the day of the Lord was at hand, Paul shows that this would be preceded by the great apostasy and the revelation of the man of lawlessness, who will be overthrown by the Lord at his coming, but whose blasphemous pretensions and lying wonders will draw many to perdition because they had no love of the truth [vv 1–12]. But as God had chosen the Thessalonian Christians for salvation, Paul exhorts them to stand fast in his doctrine, and prays that both the Father and the Son may comfort their hearts and establish them in all goodness [vv 13–17].

V 1: **Now we beseech you, brethren, touching the coming of our Lord Jesus Christ, and our gathering together unto him; 2 to the end that ye be not quickly shaken from your mind, nor yet be troubled, either by spirit, or by word, or by epistle as from us, as that the day of the Lord is just at hand;**

Now concerning the coming of our Lord Jesus Christ and our gathering together to (meet) him, (Hendriksen) Paul now turns to the main purpose of the letter, which is to correct a mistaken belief in the immediacy of Christ's second advent and the assembling to meet him [I *Thess* 4.17], and to check the neglect of present duty that this teaching had fostered at Thessalonica [2 *Thess*

3.6–15]. And since such errors in doctrine can never be expected to promote *right behaviour*, but the contrary, it is not pedantic to insist upon the practical importance of cherishing the *right beliefs*!

we request you, brothers, not to be easily shaken from your (normal state of) mind or disturbed, either by spirit or by word or by letter as from us, to the effect that the day of the Lord has arrived. (Hendriksen) Paul is concerned to counter the highly undesirable effects produced by the sensational announcement that 'the day of the Lord' (the period including the events of the end-time) had already arrived, and so the coming of Jesus could be expected at any moment! This had thrown some of the Thessalonians off balance, causing a loss of mental stability which left them in a continuing state of nervous excitement. The faint-hearted felt unfit to meet the Lord, while the idle took it as an excuse to stop work. They must not thus be swept away from sanity by these 'any-moment' adventists who falsely claim his authority for such teaching, whether it purports to be an inspired interpretation or a reported statement of his doctrine, or perhaps even a written communication [cf 3.17] – a blanket denial which possibly reflects the apostle's own uncertainty of the source of the error. It should be remembered that throughout this notoriously difficult passage Paul is motivated by a purely pastoral purpose. He does not set out to gratify an unlawful curiosity, but deliberately limits his instruction to what is necessary to correct the enthusiasts and to encourage the fearful. Indeed it is only as we realize that prophecy was never intended to provide us with a blueprint of the future that we shall avoid falling into the very error these verses were intended to prevent.

*V*3: **let no man beguile you in any wise: for** *it will not be***, except the falling away come first, and the man of sin be revealed, the son of perdition, 4 he that opposeth and exalteth himself against all that is called God or that is worshipped; so that he sitteth in the temple of God, setting himself forth as God.**

Let no one deceive you in any way whatever: (Frame) Whether this dangerous delusion is propagated in ways already mentioned [*v* 2] or in any other way, Paul emphatically warns the Thessalonians not to be deceived by it [cf *Matt* 24.4]. 'The doctrine that the day of the Lord had set in was a deception; whatever might be the motives of those who taught it, it was a perilous error and they were to guard against being its dupes' (Eadie).

for (the day of the Lord will not be present) unless first of all there comes the apostasy and there be revealed the man of lawlessness, the son of perdition, (Frame) As the clause beginning with 'for' remains unfinished, the bracketed words have to be supplied from *v* 2 to make up the sense. There was no factual basis for the agitation at Thessalonica because that day must be preceded by the apostasy and the appearance of the man of lawlessness. *The* apostasy – seemingly a subject in which they had received previous instruction [*v* 5] – is the last great religious revolt that is to culminate in the revelation of the one in whom the creature's opposition to God will reach its culmination (cf *Gen* 3.5]. Thus the final apostasy of mankind prepares the way for the manifestation of this monstrous figure, the satanically inspired human agent who fully deserves the doom announced by the title 'son of perdition', because in him all wickedness will be summed up [*v* 8]. As Vos well says, This should warn us 'not to take for granted an uninterrupted progress of the cause of Christ through all ages on toward the end. As the reign of truth will be gradually extended, so the power of evil will gather force towards the end. The making all things right and new in the world depends not on gradual amelioration but on the final interposition of God'.

he that opposeth and exalteth himself against all that is called God or that is worshipped; Paul's dependence upon Daniel is evident in this description of the activity of the Arch-enemy, whose blasphemous hostility to God was foreshadowed in the desecration of the Jews' Temple in 168 B.C. by Antiochus Epiphanes in whom the prophecy received its first fulfilment [cf *Dan* 7.25; 8.11; 11.31, 36ff; 12.11]. The phrase, 'that is called God', includes all the so-called gods of the heathen [cf 1 *Cor* 8.5], while 'or that is worshipped' embraces every object of worship held sacred by men. Carried forward by an impressive display of Satanic power (*v* 9], the man who is marked by absolute lawlessness will thus recognize no God but himself.

so that he seats himself in the sanctuary of God, proclaiming himself to be God. (Hendriksen) Although Antiochus, who erected an altar to Zeus in the Jewish Temple, and Caligula, who attempted to set up an image of himself there in A D 40, both asserted their divinity, yet the ultimate enormity of an exclusive claim to deity is reserved for the man of sin. Since under the New Covenant no special significance is attached to a particular place of worship [*John* 4.21], it is unnecessary to assume a literal reference to the adversary's entrance into any earthly 'sanctuary' whether Jewish or Christian. 'The "sitting in the temple of God" only sums up in one terse image that unholiest offence offered to the Holiest of Beings' (Vos).

What Paul is in fact saying is that this evil person will arrogate to himself the divine status and homage that belongs to God alone. This means that the Lawless One will not be content to masquerade as the Messiah, for such an outright act of self-deification precludes that professed submission to the will of God which this rôle would demand.

V5: Remember ye not, that, when I was yet with you, I told you these things?

We, alas, cannot recall Paul's oral instruction, and therein lies our difficulty! If therefore the interpretation of this passage is beset by many obscurities, it is because we 'have not the key to the cypher with which the Thessalonians had been supplied' (Adeney). If it is legitimate to link 1 John 2.18 with this verse, it would seem that the teaching that *Anti-christ*, as opposed to the many anti-christs already at work [cf *v* 7], must make his appearance before the end formed part of the general apostolic tradition [cf *v* 15]. The fact that Paul repeatedly told the Thessalonians of the events which must *precede* Christ's coming implies reproof that an intelligent grasp of his teaching had not been reflected in their conduct. They should not have been misled by the delusion that the day of the Lord had set in. The apostle's exceptional lapse into the first person singular at this point [cf 3.16] shows that he is very well aware of what he himself had taught. Probably this jogging of their memory was also intended to avoid 'further explanation in writing on a subject bordering on politics, the more explicit treatment of which might have exposed the missionaries to a renewal in more dangerous form of the charges that led to their expulsion from Thessalonica: see *Acts* 17.6f.' (Findlay).

*V*6: **And now ye know that which restraineth, to the end that he may be revealed in his own season. 7 For the mystery of lawlessness doth already work: only *there is* one that restraineth now, until he be taken out of the way.**

And you know what is restraining him now so that he may be revealed in his time. For the mystery of lawlessness is already at work; only he who now restrains it will do so until he is out of the way. (RSV)
The Thessalonians *knew* what Paul meant; we can only suggest what seems to be the most reasonable interpretation of this cryptic utterance. The mystery of lawlessness is already at work, says Paul, but *something* [*v* 6] or *someone* [v 7] is at present restraining the man of lawlessness until the appointed season for his manifestation (or appearing) has arrived. If it be asked what so restrains the forces of lawlessness, the answer then as now is probably the *rule of law* [*v* 6] as this *principle is personified* [*v* 7] in well-ordered government [cf *Rom* 13.1–6]. Not only would it have been dangerous for Paul to have spoken more plainly of the removal of Roman rule, but the intervening centuries since the disappearance of that Empire have also proved that his vague allusion to the Restrainer was far more appropriate then any specific reference to the contemporary scene. Nor was this accidental, for like all prophets inspired of God, the apostle spoke better than he knew at the time. What we have here is an example of that foreshortened perspective which is peculiar to the prophet's vision. Paul is able to set forth the events of the end-time, but he does not know or pretend to know *when* these things will take place [cf *Acts* 1.7]. So with regard to the revelation of the Arch-enemy, he 'did not see whether ten or ten thousand years were involved' (Lenski). However, the purpose of the

prophecy is not to provide believers with a time-table. It is to let them see that not even Satan's final master-stroke is an independent development. Indeed it assures them that nothing is beyond the control of the sovereign God who makes all things work together for the good of his people [*Rom* 8.28]. Meanwhile the Thessalonians can perceive that 'the mystery of lawlessness' is already secretly at work. 'Already' marks the imminence of the end, for Christians belong to the eschatological period in which the gospel mystery of salvation [1 *Tim* 3.16] is opposed by this sinister mystery of evil whose content is lawlessness. As therefore the Lawless One will rule only when the restraint of law is removed, so the precursor of his appearing will be the increase of lawlessness.

*V*8: **And then shall be revealed the lawless one, whom the Lord Jesus shall slay with the breath of his mouth, and bring to nought by the manifestation of his coming;**

After the removal of the restraining power, *then* the Lawless One will be revealed. Without pausing to say whether the period of his ascendancy will be long or short, Paul passes at once to his complete defeat at the very moment of the Lord's appearing. For the apostle's object is not to stimulate interest in the chronology of lawlessness, but to encourage the certain expectation of Christ's ultimate triumph over all the powers of evil. As Findlay points out, '*Jesus*, the human Name, could not be wanting here, where the overthrow of "the *man* of lawlessness" is in question'. This will be no protracted conflict between evenly matched antagonists, for the returning Lord will instantly slay Satan's mouth-piece and abolish all his power. The two parallel expressions that describe the destruction carry virtually the same meaning. It is fitting that 'the breath of his mouth' should be the terrible weapon with which Christ for ever silences 'this blasphemous assumer of divine prerogative' (Eadie). [cf *Is* 11.4; *Rev* 19.15]. In the second the unique combination, 'the manifestation (epiphany) of his coming (parousia)', appears to emphasize the resistless power of the Son of Man, the mere *appearing* of whose *presence* suffices to destroy his adversary.

V9: even he, **whose coming is according to the working of Satan with all power and signs and lying wonders, 10 and with all deceit of unrighteousness for them that perish; because they received not the love of the truth, that they might be saved.**

Paul now reverts to the period preceding this judgment in order to sketch the 'ministry' of Anti-christ and to emphasize its effects upon his dupes. This arch-deceiver also has an advent, he too works signs and wonders, but the infernal parody is after the pattern of Satan's working which is the way of falsehood and death [*John* 8.44]. Hence the appearance of the Lawless One will be accompanied by the supernatural *power* to perform such *signs* as will authenticate himself and make men *marvel* at him [cf *Acts* 2.22 where all three terms are used of the miracles of Christ]. The objective reality of these prodigies is not denied, but because they originate in falsehood they are teachers of lies (cf *Deut* 13.1–5). The deceit that is inspired by unrighteousness thus governs the entire manifestation of 'the son of perdition' [*v* 3], whose doom will be shared by the deluded [cf *Matt* 24.24], even 'those who are on the way to perdition'.

because they received not the love of the truth, that they might be saved. So 'because' (that is, 'in requital for their refusal': Plummer) they did not welcome the love of the truth which would have brought them salvation, they are justly given over to an infatuation with the lie which leads to their damnation [*vv* 11, 12]. 'The love of the truth', a remarkable expression which appears only here, shows that their antipathy to the truth was not so much intellectual as moral. Loving darkness rather than light [*John* 3.19], they lacked that commitment to the truth of God which issues in obedience to his will [cf 1.8]. 'Those of whom the Apostle speaks resist "the truth" with an instinctive, invincible prejudice; for they have no desire to "be saved" from the sins it condemns [*John* 3.20; cf 2 *Cor* 4.3, 4] . . . It is a just, but mournful result, that rejecters of Christ's miracles become believers in Satan's, and that atheism should be avenged by superstition. So it has been, and will be' (Findlay).

V 11: **And for this cause God sendeth them a working of error, that they should believe a lie:**

And so for this reason, it is God that sends them an energy of delusion that they may believe the falsehood; (Frame) Not for one moment will Paul leave his readers to imagine that this triumph of Satan is achieved at the expense of God's supremacy over all events. The familiar evasion that God simply 'permits' evil to exist, or that its punishment is merely the outworking of an imper-

sonal law, finds no place in the apostle's thought.[1].
Whereas it would seem from *v* 9 that Satan alone is
responsible for the success of the Lawless One in deceiving
his followers, here it is shown that God's ultimate control
over the whole process cannot be set aside. The expression
'God sends' indicates a positive, personal act [cf *Rom* 1.24,
26, 28]. It is God who sends 'an energy unto delusion'
that prepares the way for the final judgment by causing
those who rejected the truth to embrace Satan's master-lie
and worship Anti-christ (Frame). As one would expect,
the apostle faithfully adheres to the prophetic realism of
the Old Testament [cf 1 *Kings* 22.29ff; 2 *Chron* 18.18ff; *Is*
19.14; *Ezek* 14.9]. And indeed this teaching cannot be
compromised without exchanging the living God for a
finite deity, whose helplessness in the face of rampant evil
would deprive men of all comfort.

*V*12: **that they all might be judged who believed not
the truth, but had pleasure in unrighteousness.**

**in order that all may be condemned who did not
believe the truth but delighted in unrighteousness.**
(Hendriksen) Since these men had no love of the truth,
God confirmed their predilection for error by giving them
up to the lie, in order that they might receive the unfavour-

1. In a universe created and controlled by God, even the fall and all its
consequences are ordained for the furtherance of his eternal purpose.
Although this means that God is the *ultimate* cause of whatever comes to
pass, it does not make him the author of sin, because every evil act is the
result of a deliberate volition for which its *immediate* agent is responsible.
The betrayal of Jesus by Judas is probably the clearest example of this
principle of the divine government. In this, Judas remained accountable
to God though he could not have done otherwise [*Acts* 4.28], for in
yielding to the temptation of Satan he willingly followed his own evil
desires [*John* 13.27]

able verdict they deserved in the final judgment. The ground of their condemnation is twofold. So far from trusting in God's truth they did not even give credence to its testimony. They believed neither its promises nor its threatenings. This was because their preferences lay in another direction. For by resolving to take pleasure in wickedness they, like Milton's Satan, had made evil their good (Findlay). Those without 'the love of the truth' will always 'delight in unrighteousness', for between these opposite affections there is no neutral ground.

*V*13.: **But we are bound to give thanks to God always for you, brethren beloved of the Lord, for that God chose you from the beginning unto salvation in sanctification of the Spirit and belief of the truth: 14 whereunto he called you through our gospel, to the obtaining of the glory of our Lord Jesus Christ.**

From the doom that awaits the rebels, Paul turns with relief to the very different destiny which is assured to the Thessalonians by grace. His virtual repetition of the words of 1.3 seems intended to stress the fact that he and his fellow-labourers feel bound to give thanks continually for what God has wrought in them, despite the doubts voiced by the faint-hearted! For the welcome they gave to the truth not only made them their 'brethren', but also showed them to be 'beloved of the Lord' (i.e. Christ; cf *Deut* 33.12 which refers to Jehovah). Denney calls this thanksgiving 'a system of theology in miniature', because it 'covers the whole work of salvation from the eternal choice of God to the obtaining of the glory of our Lord Jesus Christ in the world to come'.

for that God chose you from the beginning unto

salvation i.e. from eternity [cf 1 *Cor* 2.7; *Eph* 1.4; 2 *Tim* 1.9]. 'The choice of God is, from its nature, an eternal choice, though His call takes place in time, and through the preaching of the gospel. This divine and ultimate aspect and origin of human salvation the apostle rejoices to contemplate, as, rising above all human instrumentalities, weakness, and failures, it carries all back to His blessed sovereignty and His gracious self-formed purpose, and gives Him all the glory' (Eadie).

through sanctification by the Spirit and belief in the truth; (Hendriksen) When God determines the end, he also ordains the means. Hence this eternal election to salvation was realized in their sanctification *by* the Spirit and belief *in* the truth. Such trust in the truth is the evidence of having been set apart for God by his Spirit. For the human response to the gospel – in conversion [cf *John* 1.12 *and* 13] and in the walk that follows it [cf *Phil* 1.12 *and* 13] – is always the result of the divine enabling! 'We have no reason to ask what God decreed before the creation of the world in order to know that we have been elected by Him, but we find in ourselves a satisfactory proof of whether He has sanctified us by His Spirit and enlightened us to faith in His Gospel' (Calvin).

to which (salvation) he also called you through our gospel, with a view to obtaining the glory of our Lord Jesus Christ. (Hendriksen) This is at once a reminder of the call of God which came to them through the preaching of the gospel, and an encouragement to persevere to glory. As the remembrance of the awakening call evokes gratitude, so the prospect of the promised consummation inspires hope [v 16]. The glory of Christ 'is the glory which Christ possesses, and which he shares [cf *Rom* 8.17] with "the beloved of the Lord". In other words, *whom he called . . . them he also glorified* [*Rom* 8.30]' (Frame).

*V*15: **So then, brethren, stand fast, and hold the traditions which ye were taught, whether by word, or by epistle of ours.**

'So then' points to a logical conclusion. Paul wants the Thessalonians to see what kind of response this understanding of God's gracious purpose should constrain. Instead of being shaken from the faith by wild rumours [*v* 2], they are to 'stand fast' in it. The resolve to remain fixed on the rock of revelation is important if one wishes to avoid finishing in the quicksands of speculation.

and hold the traditions which ye were taught, This is not another exhortation; it rather defines the call to stand fast. They would maintain the required stability only by holding fast to 'the traditions' (or teaching) they had been given. As Lightfoot notes, the prominent idea of *paradosis (tradition)* 'in the New Testament is that of an authority external to the teacher himself'. So that Paul's use of it amounts to 'a confession that he was not expressing his own ideas, but *delivering* or *handing on* a message that he had received from heaven'. [cf *Gal* 1.11, 12 and see the comment on 1 *Thess* 2.13]

whether by word, or by epistle or ours. 'Ours' qualifies what they are to hold fast, viz. the apostolic tradition, whether spoken or written [1 *Thess* 2.13]. It also implies the rejection of every other teaching as lacking the authority to command the consciences of men [cf *Col* 2.16ff]. And though we cannot now hear Paul preach in person, this tradition has been faithfully transmitted to us in the pages of the New Testament.

*V*16: **Now our Lord Jesus Christ himself, and God our Father who loved us and gave us eternal comfort and good hope through grace, 17 comfort your hearts and establish them in every good work and word.**

Now may he, our Lord Jesus Christ and God our Father, (Hendriksen) Paul now turns to prayer in order to invoke the divine blessing, without which the preceding exhortation could find no fulfilment in the lives of his converts. The fact that the name of Christ is here placed first serves to emphasize his equality with the Father [cf 2 *Cor* 13.14]. This is possibly because the immediate context has had Christ's triumph over the Lawless One so much in view.

who loved us and gave us eternal comfort and good hope through grace, Probably these words ought to be referred to the Father's great act of love in giving his Son to die for us [cf *John* 3.16], for this 'act is the source of all our consolation and hope' (Lightfoot). Believers enjoy the 'eternal comfort' which will outlast time itself, because they have embraced that 'good hope' whose glorious fulfilment will outmatch their highest expectations. All this is theirs through the supreme gift of God's grace. 'Though the cross of Christ is never mentioned in the two Letters, and His death but twice [1 *Thess* 4.14; 5.10] in cursory fashion, "the grace of God" therein displayed furnishes the basis and fulcrum of the entire system of doctrine and life in the Epistles' (Findlay).

comfort your hearts and establish them in every

good work and word. Paul's petition on their behalf is short but comprehensive in its scope. He prays that their hearts (or the inner man as seen by God) may be strengthened and settled to do good in all they do or say. For those who cherish a good hope must be seen to live good lives.

CHAPTER THREE

*Paul requests the Thessalonians to pray for the spread of the gospel
and that he and his companions might be delivered from the
persecutors who hindered their work [vv 1, 2]. He assures them
of the faithfulness of God, expresses his confidence in their
obedience, and prays for their continued progress [vv 3–5]. He
next censures the idlers, and requires the rest to withdraw from the
company of any brother who refuses to work, so that he may be
shamed into mending his ways [vv 6–15]. After a final prayer for
his readers, Paul guarantees the authenticity of the letter by adding
the closing words in his own handwriting [vv 16–18].*

*V*1: **Finally, brethren, pray for us, that the word of
the Lord may run and be glorified, even as also** *it is*
**with you; 2 and that we may be delivered from
unreasonable and evil men; for all have not faith.**

'Finally' (or 'for the rest', cf 1 *Thess* 4.1) introduces the
apostle's treatment of the important practical issues with
which the Epistle concludes. But first he asks for a place
in their prayers. As ever, he seeks nothing for himself; his
sole desire is to see the word of the Lord spread swiftly
[*Ps* 147.15] and be glorified [*Acts* 13.48] in the lives of
those who joyfully receive it.

even as also *it is* **with you;** As the original lacks a verb, it is not certain whether Paul refers to the success of their first mission ('as it did among you': RSV), or also intends to include the present progress of the gospel in Thessalonica. Be that as it may, the difficulties that faced him at Corinth doubtless made him long for the word to run as rapidly through Achaia as it had done in Macedonia.

and that we may be delivered from unreasonable and evil men; With this triumph of the word in view, they should also pray that its heralds may not be hindered from spreading it by the opposition of certain (= 'the') perverse and wicked men. The apostle clearly has a definite group in mind, which it is not hard to identify. He is thinking of the fanatical attempts of the unbelieving Jews to block the advance of the gospel at Corinth [cf *Acts* 18.5–17].

for all have not faith. Such implacable hostility to the gospel sadly shows that all men have not faith. Paul is not here stating the obvious; he is in fact explaining what lies behind the activity of these evil men. For as faith puts a man in possession of all the blessings of the world to come, so the lack of it is the mark of belonging to the present evil age. Hence when those without faith exhibit their enmity towards the truth, this antagonism is completely in accord with their nature and their destiny.

*V*3: **But the Lord is faithful, who shall establish you, and guard you from the evil *one*.**

Against the persecutors who lack 'faith' stands the 'faithful' Lord (Christ) who will keep his trusting people from being overwhelmed by these assaults, which are really instigated by the Evil One himself. By turning so abruptly from his own trials in Corinth to the dangers which threatened the Thessalonians, Paul shows that he is more concerned about them than he is about himself (Calvin). He therefore assures them of the Lord's strengthening and protecting grace. With regard to the situation in Thessalonica, this guarding will prevent them 'from falling into the snares of the evil one, such as fanaticism, loafing, meddlesomeness, neglect of duty, defeatism (see verses 5–8)' (Hendriksen).

*V*4: **And we have confidence in the Lord touching you, that ye both do and will do the things which we command.**

Having reminded his friends of the faithfulness of the Lord, Paul tactfully prepares the way for what is to follow [*v* 6] by expressing his confidence in their obedience. However, this trust in his converts is not a vote of confidence in human nature! It is a confidence which he has 'in the Lord'. Because he sees in their present obedience the evidence of divine grace at work in their lives, he also expects that they 'will do' (this has some emphasis) what he is about to lay upon them with all the authority of an apostle of Christ.

*V*5: **And the Lord direct your hearts into the love of God, and into the patience of Christ.**

However, may the Lord incline your hearts to a sense of God's love and to the endurance that Christ alone inspires. (Frame) But before Paul begins to admonish the idlers, he commends them all to the Lord (Christ) in this brief but beautiful prayer. For though he has confidence in the Lord that they will do what he commands, 'yet he is certain that the help of the Lord is indispensable to incline their hearts to keep his commandments' (Frame). There-fore he prays that they may be given such a sense of God's love to them that they will want to make his will their own; and that they may manifest the steadfast endurance that Christ alone can inspire.

*V*6: **Now we command you, brethren, in the name of our Lord Jesus Christ, that ye withdraw yourselves from every brother that walketh disorderly, and not after the tradition which they received of us.**

It is because the Thessalonians are 'brethren' that Paul claims the right to command them 'in the name of', that is, on the authority of 'the Lord Jesus Christ', whose apostle he is. This peremptory address, which was prompted by their failure to heed his milder admonition in the previous letter [1 *Thess* 4.11, 12] charges the whole community with the responsibility of disciplining the few who refused to earn their daily bread.

that you hold aloof from every brother walking in disorderly fashion, (Findlay) The loyal majority are commanded to hold aloof from every brother who 'breaks the ranks' by stopping work on the excuse that the Lord's advent is near. At least this means that they must not condone his idleness by supplying him with free food, but it may also imply his exclusion from the Lord's Supper. These measures are intended to make him mend his ways [*v* 14]; they do not amount to excommunication, for the rest of the congregation is still to regard and admonish him as 'a brother' [*v* 15].

and not in accordance with the tradition which you received from us. (Findlay) As this disobedient idleness was a serious breach of apostolic discipline, to regard it with complacency would contaminate the whole church. It was contrary to the express instruction given when Paul was with them [*v* 10] and reiterated in the first Epistle [1 *Thess* 4.11, 12; 5.14]. On 'tradition' see comment on 2.13. Although 'they' (ASV) is favoured by textual critics, 'you' (RSV, NEB) makes much better sense here.

*V*7: **For yourselves know how ye ought to imitate us: for we behaved not ourselves disorderly among you;**

The Thessalonians do not need to be told of the obligation to earn their own living, for the teaching they were given had also been conspicuously illustrated in the self-denying lives of their instructors [*v* 8]. 'Disorderly', a military term, was applied to soldiers *out of rank*. 'Officers are as much subject to discipline as the rank and file; it was due to their Churches that the Apostles should set an example of a strictly ordered life; with this example before them, which bore exactly upon the point in question, the readers "know" what the nature of their "imitation" should be' (Findlay).

*V*8: **neither did we eat bread for nought at any man's hand, but in labour and travail, working night and day, that we might not burden any of you:**

'To eat bread' is a Hebraism for gaining a living [cf *Gen* 3.19]. It seems likely from *Acts* 17.7 that the missionaries stayed with Jason, but unlike the idle brothers who were begging support from the church *they* worked to pay for their keep. Indeed they chose to accept the most exacting and incessant toil to avoid burdening the Thessalonians with their maintenance. What was said in 1 *Thess* 2.9 to prove that they did not preach for profit, is here repeated as an example to be followed by all, including the work-shy idlers!

*V*9: **not because we have not the right, but to make ourselves an ensample unto you, that ye should imitate us.**

However, Paul insists that they were entitled to claim the free support of their converts, even though they had waived that right [cf 1 *Cor* 9.12]. 'Just as Paul wanted to set an example by the work that he did, so that lazy individuals should not eat other people's food like drones, so he was unwilling that this same principle should hurt the ministers of the Word, with the result that the churches would defraud them of their lawful support' (Calvin) [1 *Tim* 5.18]

but in order that we might offer ourselves as an example for you to imitate. (Hendriksen) 'Ourselves' is thrown forward to emphasize the self-sacrifice which was involved in this waiving of their right to support. These words would make the readers shamefully recall the cost of this mission to the preachers, as they now learned that this unnecessary burden was gladly shouldered to provide them with an example of industry [cf 1 *Thess* 2.9]. 'The new religion did not teach "the dignity of labour". What it inculcated was just the duty of work' (Adolf Harnack).

*V*10: **For even when we were with you, this we commanded you, If any will not work, neither let him eat.**

For also, when we were with you, this we used to command you: 'If any one refuses to work, neither

let him eat'. (Frame) Not content to let their personal example speak for itself, the preachers had often indicated its significance by means of this crisp command. As Frame says, the 'tradition' [*v* 6] 'is not a truism: "if any one does not work, he has nothing to eat", but an ethical imperative: "if any one *refuses* to work, he shall not eat" '. It is this *unwillingness* to work which is here stigmatized as a vice. Christians are not called to idleness, but to glorify God in an honourable and useful vocation. For as the following verse mournfully proves, Satan always finds work for idle hands to do! 'The church has therefore seen that this dictum abolishes all false asceticism, all unchristian disinclination to work, all fanatic exaltation above work, all self-inflicted pauperism' (Lenski).

*V*11: **For we hear of some that walk among you disorderly, that work not at all, but are busybodies.**

For we hear that some among you are conducting themselves in a disorderly manner, not busy workers but busybodies. (Hendriksen) These things [*vv* 6–10] had to be said because Paul and his co-workers have heard that the church is being troubled by a known but unnamed minority, whose disorderly conduct is here condemned in a telling play on words. Such persons are not the *busy workers* they ought to be, but have become the *busybodies* they ought not to be! Unmindful of their own duty [cf 1 *Tim* 5.8], these idlers were meddling in the affairs of others, and then looking to the church to supply their needs. Believing that the Lord's return was at hand [2.2], they tried to persuade others to join them in waiting for it. In the meantime they expected to live on the charity of their less spiritual brethren who were still working!

*V*12: **Now them that are such we command and exhort in the Lord Jesus Christ, that with quietness they work, and eat their own bread.**

Paul now turns to command and exhort the idlers. This time he refers to them as those who are 'in the Lord Jesus Christ', which points to the privileges and obligations that belong to the believers. Hence it is both an acknowledgment of their standing and an appeal to live up to it. Further evidence of the apostle's tact in dealing with these offenders is seen in his choice of the indirect and impersonal address 'them that are such' (meaning 'people of this kind') in preference to 'you idlers' or even 'those idlers'. Instead of depending upon others for their keep, these persons are here commanded to live on the fruits of their *own* labours. 'With quietness' is not the opposite of the meddlesomeness mentioned in the previous verse, 'but of the feverish excitement of mind stimulated by the belief that the *Parousia* was at hand' (Frame). [Cf 1 *Thess* 4.11; 1 *Tim* 2.2]

*V*13: **But ye, brethren, be not weary in well-doing.**

As for the rest who have obeyed the tradition, Paul urges them not to become weary 'in well-doing', i.e. 'in your honourable course' (Lightfoot). [cf *Gal* 6.9] The reference is quite general and should not be restricted to the duty of almsgiving. The meaning within the context is well expressed by Hendriksen: 'Do not be misled. Do not let a few people who neglect *their* duty keep *you* from doing *yours*. Never grow tired of doing what is right, honourable, excellent'.

*V*14: **And if any man obeyeth not our word by this**

epistle, note that man, that ye have no company with him, to the end that he may be ashamed.

If anyone does not obey our instructions in this letter, take note of that man and do not associate with him, so that he may be ashamed of himself. (Bruce) This tells the faithful majority what to do should any one of the idlers disregard Paul's letter and persist in his disobedience. 1. They are to 'take note of that man', not by naming him publicly but by inwardly resolving to avoid him in future. 2. They are to withdraw [*v* 6] from all close association with him, 'so that he may be ashamed of himself', i.e. 'made to turn and look into himself, and so be put to shame' (Fausset). The realization of his shame would thus lead to the reformation of his conduct and his restoration to the full fellowship of the church.

*V*15: **And *yet* count him not as an enemy, but admonish him as a brother.**

This shows the spirit in which this discipline was to be carried out. He was not to be regarded as an enemy, but admonished as a 'brother'. The false idea that Christ's return was imminent had led him to neglect his immediate duty, 'but he was still to be counted a brother, as he had not forsaken the faith, or cut himself off from communion by notorious immorality, or by a relapse into heathen creed and profligacy'. Hence he was to be dealt with kindly; 'undue severity was to be avoided, the purpose being not to frown him away, but to win him back' (Eadie).

*V*16: **Now the Lord of peace himself give you peace at all times in all ways. The Lord be with you all.**

With the recognition that these prescriptions to promote the peace of the church will avail nothing without the divine blessing, Paul concludes with the prayer that Christ, the Lord of peace [*Col* 1.20] may give them 'peace at all times in all ways'. Clearly this includes far more than outward concord. He is praying that in every circumstance of life they may have an abiding sense of that peace which alone ensures the spiritual prosperity of the whole man (Morris).

The Lord be with you all. As in *v* 18, Paul includes the 'disorderly brethren', 'who even more than others need the control of "the Lord" and the calming effect of his "peace". In the Benedictions of 1 *Cor* 16.24, 2 *Cor* 13.13, *all* has the like pointed significance' (Findlay).

V 17: **The salutation of me Paul with mine own hand, which is the token in every epistle: so I write.**

The greeting by the hand of me Paul; this fact is a token of genuineness in every letter; this is the way I write. (Frame) Like his contemporaries, it was Paul's habit to dictate his letters to an amanuensis and then add the concluding greeting in his own handwriting.[1] As is the case here, he sometimes calls attention to this personal touch in order to attest the genuineness of the Epistle [cf 1 *Cor* 16.21; *Gal* 6.11; *Col* 4.18; and *Philemon* 19, though he probably wrote the whole of this himself]. In this instance it was added because of the uncertainty that is hinted at in

1. Frame refers to Deissmann's reproduction of a letter dated September 13, 50 A.D., from one Mystarion to a priest, in which the *farewell* and the date are written in another hand, a circumstance that 'proves that somebody at that date (about the time of our letter) closed a letter in his own hand without expressly saying so'.

2.2, and to show the Thessalonians that no letter which purported to come from him was to be received as authentic without his characteristic autograph [*Gal* 6.11]. This proof of authenticity would also prevent any erring member from disputing the apostolic origin of the preceding injunctions. Although 'every letter' suggests that Paul wrote many more letters than have come down to us [cf 1 *Cor* 5.9], this should cause us no concern, as we possess as many as God intended us to have. Enough indeed to show us the way of salvation and lead us to heaven!

*V*18: **The grace of our Lord Jesus Christ be with you all.**

As always Paul commends his readers to the grace that is theirs in the Lord Jesus Christ. Those who but a short time before had been heathens and whose Christian course since then had been far from easy, are here reminded once more of the all-sufficient grace of their Saviour. 'Although he has left them, they are not really alone. The free love of God, which visited them at first uncalled, will be with them still, to perfect the work it has begun. It will beset them behind and before; it will be a sun and a shield to them, a light and a defence. In all their temptations, in all their sufferings, in all their moral perplexities, in all their despondencies, it will be sufficient for them. There is not any kind of succour which a Christian needs which is not to be found in the grace of the Lord Jesus Christ' (Denney).

Soli Deo Gloria

BIBLIOGRAPHY

Adeney, Walter F., *Thessalonians and Galatians* (Century Bible) (T. C. & E. C. Jack, 1902)

Arndt, W. F. – Gingrich, F. W., *A Greek-English Lexicon of the New Testament* (University of Chicago Press, 1957)

Berkhof, L., *Systematic Theology* (Banner of Truth, 1959)

Best, Ernest, *The First and Second Epistles to the Thessalonians* (BNTC) (A & C Black, 1972)

Bicknell, E. J., *I & II Thessalonians* (WC) (Methuen, 1932)

Bruce, F. F., *I & II Thessalonians* (NBC revised) (IVP, 1970)

Bruce, F. F., *An Expanded Paraphrase of the Epistles of Paul* (Paternoster Press, 1965)

Calvin, John, *I & II Thessalonians* (St. Andrew Press, 1961, translated by Ross Mackenzie)

Cullmann, Oscar, *The Early Church* (SCM, 1976)

Denney, James, *The Epistles to the Thessalonians* (EB) (Hodder & Stoughton, 1892)

Eadie, John, *The Epistles to the Thessalonians* (James and Klock, 1977)

Ellicott, C. J., *The Epistles to the Thessalonians* (Zondervan, 1957)

Erdman, Charles R., *The Epistles of Paul to the Thessalonians* (Westminster Press, 1966)

Fausset, A. R., *I & II Thessalonians* (JFB) (Collins, 1874)

Fergusson, James, *The Epistles of Paul* (Banner of Truth, 1978)

Findlay, G. G., *The Epistles to the Thessalonians* (CBSC) (CUP, 1891)

Findlay, G. G., *The Epistles to the Thessalonians* (CGT) (CUP, 1904)

Frame, James, E., *The Epistles to the Thessalonians* (ICC) (T & T Clark, 1912)

Grier, W. J., *The Momentous Event* (Banner of Truth, 1970)

Guthrie, Donald, *New Testament Introduction* (Tyndale, 1970)

Hendriksen, William, *I & II Thessalonians* (NTC) (Banner of Truth, 1972)

Hughes, Archibald, *A New Heaven and a New Earth* (Marshall, Morgan & Scott, 1958)

Lenski, R. C. H., *I & II Thessalonians* (Augsburg, 1961)

Lightfoot, J. B., *Notes on the Epistles of St. Paul* (Zondervan, 1957)

Meeter, John E. (Editor), *The Shorter Writings of B. B. Warfield* Vol. I (Presbyterian & Reformed, 1970)

Moffatt, James, *I & II Thessalonians* (EGT) (Eerdmans, 1974)

Milligan, George, *St. Paul's Epistles to the Thessalonians* (Macmillan, 1908)

Morris, Leon, *I & II Thessalonians* (TNTC) (Tyndale, 1956)

Morris, Leon, *I & II Thessalonians* (NIC) (Eerdmans, 1959)

Neil, William, *The Epistles of Paul to the Thessalonians* (MNTC) (Hodder & Stoughton, 1950)

Plummer, Alfred, *A Commentary on St. Paul's First Epistle to the Thessalonians* (Robert Scott, 1918)

Plummer, Alfred, *A Commentary on St. Paul's Second Epistle to the Thessalonians* (Robert Scott, 1918)

Poole, Matthew, *A Commentary on the Holy Bible*, Vol. III (Banner of Truth, 1963)

Ridderbos, Herman, contributor to *Revelation and the Bible* (Tyndale, 1965)

Tasker, R. V. G., *The Biblical Doctrine of the Wrath of God* (Tyndale, 1970)

Trapp, John, *Commentary on the New Testament* (Sovereign Grace Book Club, 1958)

Trench, R. C., *Synonyms of the New Testament* (James Clarke, 1961)

Vincent, Marvin R., *Word Studies in the New Testament* (Macdonald, n.d.)

BIBLIOGRAPHY

Vine, W. E., *Expository Dictionary of New Testament Words* (Oliphants, 1958)

Vos, Geerhardus, *The Pauline Eschatology* (Baker Book House, 1979)

Vos, Geerhardus, *Redemptive History and Biblical Interpretation* (Presbyterian & Reformed, 1980)

Warfield, B. B., *Biblical and Theological Studies* (Presbyterian & Reformed, 1952)

Warfield, B. B., *Perfectionism* (Presbyterian & Reformed, 1958)